Low-Carbon Investing
Defending the Climate
Emphasizing Performance

A Practical Guide for Busy Investors

J. Patrick Costello, CFP®, CLU

2018

Low-Carbon Investing
Defending the Climate Emphasizing Performance
A Practical Guide for Busy Investors

Printed in the United States of America

Second Printing, 2018

ISBN 978-0-9853364-1-7

GreenWorld Publishing
321 San Anselmo Avenue
San Anselmo, CA 94960

Library of Congress Control Number: 2018908601

We do not inherit the earth from our ancestors,
we borrow it from our children.

Fear not, my friends!
Investors who strategically embrace the transition to a
low-carbon, sustainable economy shall be rewarded.

CONTENTS

J. Patrick Costello, CFP®, CLU
CA Insurance License #0B33627
Certified Financial Planner™
Chartered Life Underwriter

Green River Sustainable Financial Services
321 San Anselmo Avenue
San Anselmo, CA 94960
PH: (415) 453-6000
FAX: (415) 520-0299
CELL: (415) 710-3978
EMAIL: PCostello@ProtectedInvestors.com

nvestments in stocks, bonds, mutual funds, and exchange-traded funds are subject to market risk, including the loss of principal invested. Investors should carefully consider their investment objectives, their risk tolerance and the individual risk/reward attributes of any fund, individual stock or bond instrument considered for investment. Additionally, before investing in a fund, investors should read the fund prospectus carefully and make sure they understand the risks and objectives of the fund, as well as the internal fund costs and potential transaction costs when buying or selling shares of the Fund. Fund prospectuses are available online from the fund company offering the fund, or by mail if requested.

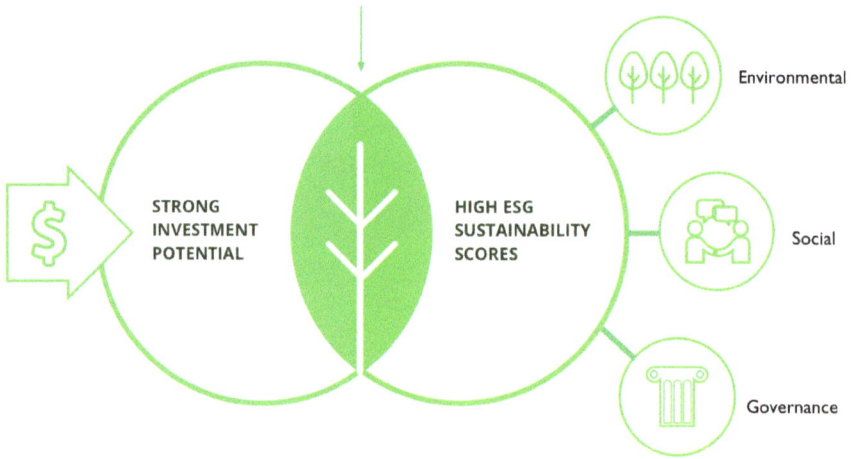

OPTIMAL SPACE FOR SUSTAINABLE INVESTORS
Companies considered for investment

STRONG
INVESTMENT
POTENTIAL

HIGH ESG
SUSTAINABILITY
SCORES

Environmental

Social

Governance

PROLOGUE

This book is intended for the everyday investor, as a resource guide to Sustainable, Low-Carbon, ESG investing, focused mainly on the use of funds — "baskets" of stocks and bonds — for personal investment.

It will be less useful for people interested in the minutia of individual stock or bond selection. Funds are often the most appropriate investment vehicle for investors because of their ease of use, holdings transparency and diversification attributes. More on this later!

Within this book, the reader will find several different but related elements. First, it includes an overview of the current state of Sustainable, "ESG" investing.

Secondly, it delivers the key message that evaluating corporations for investment potential by scrutinizing their Environmental, Social and Governance practices can do more than identify companies that are good corporate citizens — it can lead to excellent investment outcomes.

The center of the book serves as an investor's guide covering the basics of investing, particularly the "how" and the "why" of investment portfolio construction. We focus on the tools and strategies Financial Planners use to build portfolios that reflect the individual's unique circumstances and tolerance for investment risk.

Finally, from the perspective of a practicing Certified Financial Planner™, this book shows investors how to navigate the obstacles and opportunities of the financial services industry, helping them see through industry propaganda and misinformation and steer clear of conflicts of interest to find the resources they need to become successful Green, Low-Carbon investors.

2018 UPDATE

An earlier version of this book was published in 2013 to present individual investors with several fundamental facts:

1 Sustainable, Socially Responsible, ESG investing does not require financial sacrifice, nor an undue amount of extra research
2 Big financial firms and legacy fund families may **not** be the best "partners" for investors pursuing Sustainable, Low-Carbon investing

The Green, Sustainable Investing world has grown tremendously during the past five years, and the statements cited above have been amplified and continue to be validated.

There has also been a significant increase in the quantity and quality of online resources available to aspiring sustainable, low-carbon investors.

Despite this rapid evolution in sustainable investing, the information I set out to provide five years ago remains relevant and useful to the investors of today.

Most of the 2013 text is left as originally written. I'll use this 2018 update section to point out new investor resources and elements of the original text that need to be updated.

NOMENCLATURE AND ACRONYMS: "Green Investing," "Sustainable Investing" and "Socially Responsible Investing" are broad terms, meant to serve as overarching descriptors for investment practices that seek to balance the investor's profit motive with a desire to do good in the world.

One of the new conventions in sustainable investing is the emergence of an acronym — "ESG," used to specify the threefold set of criteria sustainable investors use to evaluate corporate behavior and make investment decisions.

E, S and G represent:

- Environmental impact
- Social environment for employees
- Governance practices of the Corporation

It's important to note that ESG analysis does not replace traditional investment processes, it augments them! Another way to explain this is to say that first, sustainable fund managers create a universe of successful companies appropriate to their investing niche. Then ESG analysis is applied to separate the (sustainable) wheat from the proverbial chaff.

In their marketing piece called "Spotlight on ESG Criteria," the Pax World fund family describes their process as "The full integration of environmental, social and governance (ESG) factors into investment analysis and portfolio construction."

Pax believes ESG factors have financial impact on corporate performance, and that integrating these factors into portfolio management can mitigate risk and add value to a portfolio. They believe the ESG process helps them, as fund managers, choose stocks and bonds from better-managed companies that:

- are industry leaders;
- uphold high standards of corporate responsibility and sustainability with all stakeholders;
- focus more on long term results.

To drill down a little further, the ENVIRONMENTAL component of ESG analysis examines a company's approach to climate change, emissions from operations and resource efficiency. The SOCIAL component includes an assessment of workplace diversity, employee culture, and product integrity and safety. GOVERNANCE considerations include board of director and executive diversity, corporate decision-making transparency, and the executive compensation process.

ENVIRONMENT

Protection of the Environment

ESG

Accountable Diverse Corporate Governance

Employee Social Culture

GOVERNANCE   **SOCIAL**

In 2013, the acronym in vogue was "SRI," representing Socially Responsible Investing. Realistically, ESG and SRI are nearly interchangeable. Sustainable investors may have adopted "ESG" to get away from values laden language like "Socially Responsible," and focus on the science and rigorous data analysis incorporated into today's sustainability analysis. So please, as you read the original text, translate "SRI" as a warmer, fuzzier way to describe "ESG" investing!

SUSTAINABLE, ESG INVESTING PERFORMANCE VERIFIED: In 2013 I cited studies, articles and fund performance data affirming the absence of a performance "penalty" paid by sustainable investors.

Over the past five years, a raft of additional studies prove beyond doubt that sustainable, ESG analysis does not hurt investment results; in fact it may enhance them!

Sustainable, ESG analysis may enhance investment results.

Several of the most recent studies are included in Appendix A at the back of the book.

Two of the articles — *"Sustainable Investing Research Suggests No Performance Penalty"* (11-10-2016), and *"Does Sustainable Investing Hurt or Help Returns?"* (12-07-2017) — were written by John Hale, Ph.D., CFA, and published by Morningstar, the independent fund assessment organization.

One article — *"Funds That Can Put Your Investments on a Low-Carbon Diet" (10-13-2017)* was published in the New York Times.

A fourth article — *"Sustainable Reality: Understanding the Performance of Sustainable Investing Strategies" (March, 2015)* was published by the Morgan Stanley Institute for Sustainable Investing.

Sustainable investing advocates no longer need to spend time defending the performance question. It's time to move on to other topics, such as:

- The persistent (but improving) lack of visibility of many sustainable fund families **within employer retirement plans**, and
- The continuing need for more asset class diversity. For example, there are still very few sustainable "Emerging Market" stock or bond funds available. (Countries considered 'Emerging' represent the fasting growing economies in the world — China, India, Brazil, Indonesia, etc.). "EM" funds are an important element of a properly diversified portfolio.

What Else Is New Since 2013?

SIZE MATTERS: Most important has been the startling increase in the amount of US wealth managed sustainably.

According to the bi-annual 2016 Report on Sustainable, Responsible and Impact Investing Trends, published by The Forum for Sustainable and Responsible Investment (US SIF), the market size of sustainable, responsible and impact investing in the United States reached $8.72 trillion in the beginning of 2016, a 33 percent increase since 2014.

By the beginning of 2016, one fifth of invested US assets were managed under the rubric of Sustainable, Socially Responsible, ESG or Impact investing. When the next report is issued for 2018, that percentage is likely to be closer to one fourth.

SUSTAINABLE, ESG INVESTING INDUSTRY NEWS: In January of 2018, Larry Fink, the CEO of Blackrock, the world's largest asset manager, published his annual letter to CEOs, and it was somewhat of a bombshell.

His rhetoric (at least) clearly supported the basic precepts of Sustainable, Low-Carbon investing. He encouraged corporate executives to position their businesses for long term profitability, to look for ways to benefit all stakeholders (not just the largest shareholders), and to seek ways for their companies to make a positive contribution to society.

Although this language lacks specifics, it does break some new ground in mainstream American corporate culture. His letter points the way forward to the day when it will be taken for granted that corporate leaders are focusing on minimizing negative environmental impacts, developing a nourishing employee culture and using commonly acknowledged best practices for corporate governance.

CONTINUED GROWTH IN 2018: Sustainable, ESG investing continues to experience accelerated growth in the first six months of 2018.

Morningstar's David Hale, Ph.D., published an article on January 4, 2018 titled "Sustainable Fund Choices Continued to Expand in

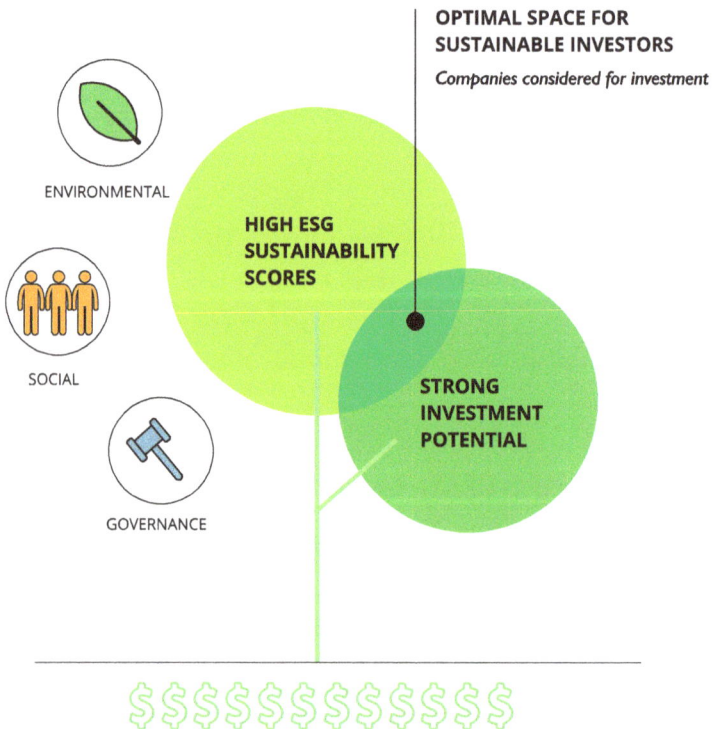

OPTIMAL SPACE FOR
SUSTAINABLE INVESTORS
Companies considered for investment

ENVIRONMENTAL

HIGH ESG
SUSTAINABILITY
SCORES

SOCIAL

STRONG
INVESTMENT
POTENTIAL

GOVERNANCE

2017." He counted a total of 39 new funds launched in 2017, as well as 17 existing funds now added to the universe that chose to add ESG metrics and analysis to their stock and bond selection process.

In July, Dr. Hale updated his numbers from 2017 to reflect 13 **new** funds being launched in the first half of 2018, as well as 28 existing funds adding ESG or impact criteria to their investment processes. He now counts 285 sustainable mutual funds and exchange traded funds available to the investing community.

For the first five months of 2018, the average monthly inflow into sustainable funds was $924 million. This was almost double the average monthly pace of $532 million in 2017.

LEGACY MUTUAL FUND FAMILIES — CAUGHT IN THE HEADLIGHTS: The biggest mutual fund families have been reluctant to embrace the rapidly growing popularity of Sustainable, ESG investing.

Of the thousands of funds these gargantuan firms manage, only a few utilize sustainability metrics when selecting stocks or bonds for their funds.

Here is a personal story that illustrates the branding and perception power exerted by multi-national financial companies that have become household names by virtue of enormous marketing budgets:

In 2016, two siblings approached me who had just recently been granted authority to manage inherited seven figure investment portfolios. They were very interested in working with a Financial Planner to lower the carbon footprint of these assets that, up until now, had been managed conventionally by a large bank's Trust department.

At an initial meeting I provided an overview of the strong relative performance and rapid growth of the sustainable investing industry.

One of the siblings looked at me skeptically and asked: "If sustainable investing performance is so strong, why have the largest fund families chosen to mostly ignore it with respect to their own funds?"

He seemed to imagine that the financial service industry had a certain purity and simplicity in which the main driver of fund family investment policy was based on achieving the best performance for fund shareholders.

I was surprised by such credulousness, knowing (as someone who majored in political science in college) that in our system of capitalism, the big corporations in every industry — not just financial services — are much more concerned with their profit margins than the quality of their products.

Large firms have also learned that marketing and branding can be used to sell inferior, high profit margin products to consumers.

But when it comes to legacy fund families grappling with their response to the growing interest in sustainable investing options, one word is extraordinarily meaningful: TAXES.

The largest fund families manage hundreds of billions of dollars for individuals, pension funds and university endowment funds. Much of this money is invested in passive Index tracking funds — funds holding the same fossil fuel stocks that appear in the S&P 500 Index, or the Dow Jones Industrial Average Index. Fund families specializing in active fund management have also held substantial amounts of fossil fuel stocks for many years, frequently touting their "strong dividends" to investors.

If these fund families begin recommending that clients move to fossil fuel-free funds, the sale of tremendous amounts of fossil fuel stocks would unleash enormous capital gains tax consequences for many of their customers. Such a transition would be awkward from a public relations standpoint, not to mention expensive and labor-intensive.

It's clear that the largest legacy mutual fund families have good reason to hesitate before aggressively recommending sustainably managed funds. But the tide is turning, and it's only a matter of time before even they will be forced to embrace sustainable investing. Why? Because their clients will demand it!

MORE SUSTAINABLE INVESTING OPTIONS WITHIN EMPLOYEE RETIREMENT PLANS: Although there is still a long way to go, the trend is pointing in the right direction. In 2018, more company retirement plans are offering sustainable fund options to their employees. To increase progress in this area, employees themselves must demand access to more ESG, low-carbon and fossil-fuel free investing options.

ASCENDENCY OF "GREEN" BONDS: Green Bonds are a rapidly growing sector of the sustainable investing marketplace. People without a lot of investing experience tend to undervalue bonds, but they play a critical role in a diversified, risk-calibrated portfolio.

Green Bonds are a rapidly growing sector of the sustainable investing marketplace.

Not only do bonds pay a declared interest rate, but when there are shocks to the stock market, bonds typically rise in value, offsetting some of the stock losses. In this way, they reduce the overall volatility of a diversified portfolio, which in turns helps investors retain confidence in their long term investing strategies.

Green bond *funds* are now available, both as mutual funds and as ETFs. A variety of corporate bonds may be selected by fund managers for a particular green bond fund, using the same ESG sustainability metrics fund families apply to stocks.

Additionally, states like California, as well as other municipalities, issue *individual green municipal bonds*, targeted to specific sustainable purposes. As of November 30, the Climate Bonds Initiative declared that California had issued $5 billion dollars of green bonds in 2017, targeted to environmentally beneficial projects.

In Europe Green bonds are issued by a wide variety of institutions, including the World Bank. They are ordinary fixed income instruments whose proceeds are predominately allocated to financing projects such as renewable energy, pollution control and energy efficiency.

Over 100 issuers, investors and underwriters updated the Green Bond Principles (GPB) in June of 2017. These are voluntary guidelines for transparency and reporting that will standardize the market and help it continue to grow. The Climate Bonds Initiative estimates total new issuance of Green Bonds in 2017 at $150 billion dollars.

SOCIAL INVESTING OPTIONS AND COMMUNITY BANKS: Social investment organizations such as Calvert Impact Capital and RSF Social Finance now permit investors to make loans to community programs while earning a modest return. Banking services that have transparent goals for community benefit investments are now increasingly available to the public.

THE ADVENT OF BENEFIT CORPORATIONS: Benefit corporations are for-profit entities that are required by law to create a material positive impact on society and the environment, in addition to earning profits for its shareholders. In other words, people are seeking to incorporate sustainability concerns into the legal structure of companies, a very positive development in the evolution of modern capitalism.

INCREASED INTEREST FROM MILLENNIALS AND RETIREES: Polls shows that millennials and young people generally are very concerned about the climate implications of their investment strategies. There is a burgeoning national movement by college students urging trustees of university endowment funds to divest from fossil fuel stocks.

Additionally, people approaching or entering retirement — particularly women — are increasingly interested in taking climate impacts and sustainability goals like executive gender balance into account when designing their own portfolios.

SUSTAINABLE INVESTING TOOLS PROLIFERATE: In the past five years, there has been a dramatic increase in the number of sustainable investing tools made available to consumers and professionals alike.

These include:

- Morningstar.com's Sustainability ratings;

- The website FossilFreeFunds.org, which allows investors to examine their funds' holdings for fossil fuel industry exposure; and
- Green(*ish*) robo-advisors, which are automated, online portfolio management services offering limited exposure to sustainably managed, low-carbon funds. Two examples are Macroclimate.com, and Aspiration.com.

"BIG DATA" IS HELPING TO DRIVE THE SURGE IN ESG, LOW-CARBON INVESTING: When professional money managers develop ESG screening protocols to evaluate companies for potential investment, they need to procure and integrate a great deal of information about corporate activities and impacts.

Some of the biggest financial data firms in the world, including MSCI, Standard and Poor's and Morningstar are competing for dominance in this arena, each hoping that their way of organizing, measuring and delivering data will become the new standard.

NEW INVESTING TOOLS FOR MANAGERS OF LARGE POOLS OF CAPITAL: *Indexes* are a measurement of the value of sections of the stock/bond market. *Index funds* are vehicles that allow investors to track a particular index with their investments.

New low-carbon and ESG indexes created by international consulting firms are now available for "benchmarking," targeted to trustees and managers of large pension funds and university endowment funds. "Benchmarking" allows trustees and actuaries of pension funds to use historical trends to make reasonably accurate projections of growth so that future retirees or other can expect to receive the benefits they were promised.

As low-carbon investment strategies are deployed by managers of these huge pools of money, important market signals are being sent, pressuring corporations to reduce their carbon footprints to make themselves more attractive to investors. Fossil fuel companies are incented to move away more rapidly from coal, oil and gas and become leaders instead of impediments in the transition to a clean energy economy.

PENSION TRUSTEES REQUIRED TO CONSIDER CLIMATE IMPACT OF INVESTMENTS: Pension Trustees in Canada and the European Union are now required to consider climate impacts from greenhouse gas emissions when evaluating pension investments. SB 964, a bill up for consideration in California's current legislative session, instructs California's Pension trustees to consider the climate-related financial risks of investments and to report on the alignment of the funds with the Paris climate agreement.

BETTER CORPORATE REPORTING: Reflected in popular acronyms such as "CSR" (Corporate Social Responsibility), or slogans such as the "Triple Bottom Line," corporate managers are eager to paint their organizations with the imprimatur of sustainability.

Undoubtedly some of what may be hastily done for PR purposes can rightly be portrayed as "green washing." However, in many cases, the CSR movement is leading to more accountability and better public access to details of corporate sustainability efforts. This can only help Sustainable, ESG investors acquire better information.

Additionally, several of the world's largest asset managers have launched efforts to get companies to disclose the risks they face from climate change. The impacts of this increased demand for assessment and disclosure have been substantial.

For the first time ever, there were majority shareholder votes on climate-risk disclosure resolutions at Exxon Mobile and Occidental Petroleum. In December of 2017, on the second anniversary of the signing of the Paris Climate Agreement, a group of global investors launched an initiative called Climate Action 100+ to drive action on climate change among 100 companies that are the world's largest greenhouse gas emitters.

SOME OTHERWISE WELL-INFORMED PEOPLE REMAIN IN THE DARK WHEN IT COMES TO SUSTAINABLE INVESTING: Twice in the last couple of years I have had to write articles critical of well-known progressive politicians who were revealed to have personal investments in fossil fuel companies.

You can still "google" my November 1, 2016 article titled "What Jill Stein Gets Wrong About Sustainable Investing." Jill Stein was the Green Party's nominee in the 2016 US Presidential election. She had been attacked and accused of hypocrisy when it was revealed that her personal investments included stocks of fossil fuel companies.

Unfortunately, she made some regrettably uninformed statements in her defense. She declared that while exploring socially responsible mutual funds, she had "…found their investments in fracking and large-scale biofuels not much better than non-green funds." This statement is simply not true and makes clear that she had not taken the time to investigate the sustainable investing industry.

Possibly she relied on the advice of a poorly informed Financial advisor. Sadly, many professionals working for large firms are focused on selling their own firm's products and are profoundly unaware of the dimensions and breadth of the sustainable investing industry, or the latest data on sustainable investing performance.

Global Warming, an Existential Threat to Humanity

During these last five years, the world community has awakened to the need to take dramatic steps to counteract the destructive impacts of global warming and its corollary, sea level rise.

The world's leading scientists have told us that reducing carbon-based greenhouse gases is imperative if we plan to honor the goals of the historic 2016 Paris

Reducing carbon-based greenhouse gases is imperative.

Climate Agreement. The fundamental goal, agreed to by 171 international signatories, is to limit global average surface temperature warming to 2 degrees Celsius — or the even more aggressive "stretch" goal of 1.5 degrees C.

These numbers are measured from a pre-industrial baseline (average temperatures recorded prior to 1850). An average surface temperature increase of 2 degrees Celsius (3.6 degrees Fahrenheit) equates roughly to a doubling of pre-industrial CO_2 levels.

How did this agreement on a maximum temperature limit emerge? Over the past couple of decades, as more data were examined, an international scientific consensus was reached. Climate scientists agree that warming of 2 degrees Celsius is the maximum threshold if the earth's climate is to remain **sustainable** for the 8 to 9 billion people projected to inhabit this wondrous "blue marble" by the end of the century.

The bad news is that even these limits may not be adequate. Many climate scientists now doubt whether the targets and voluntary commitments agreed to by the signatories to the Paris Agreement will be sufficient to keep the planet's rising temperatures — and oceans — from causing catastrophic disruptions to global populations.

Bill McKibben, founder of **350.org**, the international climate protection organization, has been writing for general audiences about the climate since 1989. In December of 2017, he published a piece in Rolling Stone magazine, titled "Winning Slowly is the Same as Losing."

He makes clear in the article why global warming is arguably the most difficult challenge faced by modern humanity.

Other problems suffered by millions of Americans such as inadequate healthcare could in time be reversed by better policy and better political leadership. Many will suffer — and are suffering - in the interim, but the problems can be solved or ameliorated in the future.

In contrast, climate scientists tell us that global warming and sea level rise, taken together, become exponentially, irreversibly worse for the entire population over time.

RECENT DATA ON GREENHOUSE GAS EMISSIONS AND GLOBAL WARMING:
June 5, 2018: The Weather Network published a story on a recent study based on 25 years of NASA and European satellite data showing how sea level rise is increasing faster than originally thought. Global warming and consequently the rapid ice melt occurring in both Greenland and Antarctica are responsible for the acceleration.

Another recent study shows that Antarctica has lost about 3 trillion tons of ice in the last 25 years, and leading ice scientists warn that coastal cities world wide could face constant flooding by the end of the century. Antarctica stores enough frozen water to raise global sea levels by almost 200 feet. Knowing how fast it is melting is of grave importance for policy makers.

The National Climate Assessment is a U.S. governmental report contributed to by over 300 experts. Among their findings are that the last three years — 2015, 2016 and 2017 have been the hottest years on record, and that snow and ice cover has decreased in most areas with the most dramatic reductions at the poles.

In fact, minimum arctic sea ice (usually during September) has decreased by more than 40%. NCA states that "This decline is unprecedented in the historical record, and the reduction of ice volume and thickness is even greater."

Greenhouse gasses and the global warming they are driving pose an enormous and accelerating threat to the ability of humanity to live comfortably on this planet.

February 26, 2018: The University of York in the U.K. published an article explaining that levels of ethane and propane in the atmosphere have been underestimated by more than 50%. These gasses escape into the air from leaks during natural gas extraction and distribution, including from fracking.

June 21, 2018: An article in US News reports that oil and gas drilling gives off far more methane (the powerful greenhouse gas) than the U.S. government has estimated previously, due to leaky wells going unnoticed by federal regulators.

A flurry of recent scientific papers indicate that governments are underestimating the economic risks of climate change, due to the use of flawed models. Many of these older climate modeling systems fail to account for "tipping points," levels of atmospheric change beyond which impacts accelerate and become unstoppable or irreversible.

The well-known "Keeling Curve" is based on scientist Charles David Keeling's CO2 measurements since 1958 at Hawaii's Mauna Loa observatory. Keeling's first readings in 1958 were at 315 ppm (parts per million). The reading just topped 410 for the month of April, 2018, a new high, and the highest number in at least 800,000 years.

THE URGENCY OF REDUCING OUR COLLECTIVE CARBON FOOTPRINT CANNOT BE OVEREMPHASIZED: Climate scientists are telling us that once global temperatures have risen far enough to hit key tipping points (such as melting polar icecaps, fundamental changes in ocean acidity, or disruptions to the paths and temperatures of major ocean currents), there may truthfully be no way to reverse course, no matter how radical the corrective actions taken after the fact.

IMPLICATIONS FOR INVESTORS: Consequently, as a long time Certified Financial Planner™, investment advisor and climate activist, something important has become clear to my clients and me:

> *The most important real-world impact of sustainable investing is the reduction of the carbon "footprint" of investor portfolios, first and foremost by divesting from fossil fuel companies.*

Divestment is the first half of the process. Once divested, investor dollars should be reinvested in companies and industries positioned to speed the development and adoption of clean energy sources and other industrial initiatives that further reduce emissions of climate-warming greenhouse gases.

By voting with our investment dollars, we are pushing the fossil-fuel majors to accelerate their pivot to cleaner energy. Ultimately it is hoped that government regulators and common sense will prevail, and these coal, oil and gas companies will leave much of their reserves unburned and in the ground, where they belong.

By voting with our investment dollars, we are pushing the fossil-fuel majors to accelerate their pivot to cleaner energy.

For the low-carbon focused financial advisor or investor, this means "de-carbonizing" investment portfolios by choosing funds that:

- Avoid investing in companies directly involved in the fossil fuel industry,
- Evaluate the full spectrum of greenhouse gas emissions from companies chosen for the fund, and when other factors are equal, opt for the companies with the lowest carbon footprint.

FOSSIL FUEL INDUSTRY DIVESTMENT VS ENGAGEMENT: There are people who feel that being a shareholder of, say, Exxon or Chevron allows them to have the proverbial seat at the table, where they can advocate for change. But frankly, advocacy, by itself, has not worked to change the fossil fuel industry.

In May of 2018, Bill McKibben, a leader of the climate movement wrote a piece for Rolling Stone, called "Hit Fossil Fuels Where It Hurts," that makes this point.

As he says, big investors — including companies that manage mutual funds and exchange traded funds — *can* use their financial clout as shareholders to lobby corporate executives to make important changes to their firms' business practices.

Sometimes important improvements in company business practices *are* achieved through this sort of shareholder advocacy.

Bill explains that this is an approach that never made much sense with the fossil fuel industry, where the flaw is not in the way they do business — <u>it resides in the business plan itself.</u>

And the history of engagement with the fossil fuel industry majors — the ones with oil and gas and coal assets that a majority of climate scientists say should never be burned - is less than inspiring.

Bill's article uses Exxon as a good case in point. About a year ago, after years of rebuffing shareholder resolutions asking them to prepare a "climate risk report," showing how the fight against global warming might stress their business model, they grudgingly agreed to do so.

New York State's Comptroller, Thomas DiNapoli was thrilled, and called a press conference to congratulate himself for the hard-won victory. Sadly, in just a few weeks, Exxon issued a report claiming that climate change posed essentially no risk to its future. They stated their intent to go on exploring for more oil while burning almost all of their existing reserves.

In a nutshell, that sort of corporate head-in-the sand attitude is why climate activists advocate for *Divestment* from fossil fuel stocks — first, because it seems to be the only message that has a chance of getting through to management, and more importantly, **because investing in an industry that is ignoring their stranded assets problem is a huge risk for investors.**

WORLDWIDE MOVEMENT AWAY FROM FOSSIL FUELS: There is a massive, growing international movement to divest from fossil fuel company stocks. Each week seems to bring news of another college, university, religious institution or private wealth fund choosing to divest from fossil fuel stocks. In July of 2018 Ireland became the first country to commit to total divestment from fossil fuel stocks within five years.

Norway is well on its way to divesting its huge 1 trillion sovereign wealth fund from fossil fuel stocks, starting with coal holdings. *This trend is irreversible* and is bound to depress fossil fuel company stock prices, and eventually affect their business practices.

As of July 9, 2018, GoFossilFree.org states that 893 institutions, representing 6 trillion dollars of accumulated wealth, are in the process of divesting from fossil fuel companies.

A group of leading economists, including James Galbraith, Juliet Schor, Jeffrey Sachs and Yanis Varoufakis recently signed a declaration calling for an immediate end to new investments in fossil fuel production and infrastructure.

On December 19th, 2017, New York governor Andrew Cuomo called on the $201.3 Billion New York State Common Retirement Fund to stop all significant fossil fuel investments.

He cited the World Bank's recent announcement that it will stop financing oil and gas exploration within two years.

New York State's employee pension fund — the third-largest in the U.S. — had holdings of at least 50 oil and gas companies that have been identified as some of the most carbon-intensive operations in the world, the governor's office said.

In the US, a number of cities and towns in California, including San Francisco, Oakland, San Mateo, Imperial Beach and Santa Cruz, in addition to Marin County, have filed climate lawsuits against fossil fuel companies.

In July of 2018, Nobel Prize winning economist Joseph Stiglitz waived his normal fee and submitted a 50-page brief to the court, supporting the children's climate lawsuit that originated during Obama's Presidency and is being handled by Our Children's Trust. He says that acting on climate change now is still manageable and would have net-negative costs. "Defendants must act with all deliberate speed and immediately cease the subsidization of fossil fuels, and any new fossil fuel projects, and implement policies to rapidly transition the U.S. economy away from fossil fuels. This urgent action is not only feasible, the relief requested will benefit the economy."

These legal actions are being taken to hold these firms financially liable for decades of greenhouse gas emissions that coal, oil, and gas company managers knew were damaging local ecosystems and infrastructure through sea level rise, pollution and rising temperatures.

Although we do not know how these legal measures will fare in court, their visibility to the public should help galvanize citizen activism and remove these companies' "social license" for continuing with business as usual.

Carbon Bubble/Stranded Assets — In June of 2018, the online magazines Cosmos and The Guardian reported on a new study in the journal "Nature Climate Change."

The study's authors observed that plunging prices for renewable energy and rapidly increasing investment in low-carbon technologies could leave fossil fuel companies with trillions in stranded assets, leading to a loss of as much as 4 trillion dollars from the international economy.

Their new conclusions suggest that regardless of regulatory impacts, which alone are substantial, energy markets will increasingly tilt toward renewable sources simply because they are cheaper and more abundant.

The study authors state that a sudden drop in demand for fossil fuels before 2035 is likely, given the current global investments and economic advantages in a low-carbon transition.

There could be a "tipping point" when this problem is suddenly fully recognized, causing the value of these companies to be recalculated and drastically lowered.

By continuing to ignore this looming problem, the world could be heading for fiscal havoc on a scale not seen since the 2008 crisis, erasing as much as $US4 trillion from the global economy, with fossil fuel industries at the center of the upheaval, and the United States, Russia and Canada tipped as big losers.

A recent paper in the journal "Nature" states that <u>fossil fuel reserves are overfunded</u>. The authors state that "globally, a third of oil reserves, half of gas reserves and over 80 per cent of current coal reserves should remain unused from 2010 to 2050 in order to meet the target of 2°C."

Environmentalists argue that <u>clean energy sources are underfunded.</u> The think tank Ceres estimates that $12.1 trillion needs to be invested in new clean power generation over the next 25 years to limit climate change to 2°C. The pace at which this happens has vast implications for the future of our climate — and for the valuation of companies that continue to rely on the burning of fossil fuels to be profitable.

A COMBINATION OF INDIVIDUAL AND COLLECTIVE ACTION IS THE SOLUTION: Individual and institutional investors can play a crucial role in the effort to defend the climate by expediting the transition to low-carbon, fossil-fuel free investing strategies.

At the same time, it's critical that citizens, institutions, governments and regulators take decisive action and mandate an accelerated move to a low-carbon economy.

DANGER AHEAD: Even investors not particularly interested in sustainability would do well to recognize the *heightened investment risk to investors holding funds containing fossil fuel company stocks*. Pension fund and university endowment fund Trustees — and future beneficiaries — should think long and hard about whether these funds should continue to own shares of fossil fuel companies.

REDUCING EMISSIONS MAKES ECONOMIC SENSE: An article in The Guardian from May 23, 2018 discussed a study led by Stanford professor Marshall Burke. The study was published in the journal Nature, and the authors estimate that the world will save $30 trillion dollars in damages, at an estimated cost of $.5 trillion dollars, by hitting the toughest Paris Accord target limiting global warming to 1.5 degrees C.

BLESSING OR CURSE? — LEGACY FIRMS ARE RUSHING TO LAUNCH "GREEN" INVESTING OPTIONS: Wall Street firms, as well as traditional fund families who just a few years ago mostly ignored the rising interest in sustainable investing, are enthusiastically launching ESG funds.

Companies like State Street Global Advisors, Nuveen, Fidelity, Van Eck, BlackRock, JPMorgan and others are suddenly competing in the sustainable investing space. Some of these new funds are narrowly focused on one element of sustainable investing.

For example, State Street Advisors (SSGA) commissioned a **Fearless Girl statue** on the first anniversary of its Gender Diversity ETF — symbol "SHE". This fund invests in companies that have a high percentage of female leadership. The statue became a major publicity coup when it was placed opposite the Wall Street bull in time for International Women's Day in early March.

Other funds have their own matrix of ESG factors and choose companies using a blended assessment of company environmental, social and governance impacts, not favoring any one of the three areas of scrutiny.

THE CHALLENGE OF FOCUSING ON LOW-CARBON AND FOSSIL-FUEL FREE INVESTING: Obviously, all sustainable investors do not share the exact same list of priorities. There are a host of ESG metrics that have meaning and importance as investors learn to use their wealth to encourage better corporate behavior. This does pose a problem for investors who are first and foremost worried about climate change, as there is no way to tell whether a fund labeled "ESG" has exposure to the fossil fuel industry, or even has a relatively low carbon footprint.

This is precisely why my investment firm Green River uses online tools to assess each fund's carbon footprint and "carbon risk" score, regardless of how the fund is described in its marketing literature.

Investors focused on a low-carbon investing strategy must go beyond a fund's label or name and run it through an online search engine such as AsYouSow's FossilFreeFunds.org, which uses a robust data bank of fund holdings to quantify and specify exactly what a fund's fossil fuel industry exposures are. This is an invaluable resource.

Financial data companies such as MSCI, Standard and Poor's and Sustainalytics are developing "carbon risk" metrics that can be very useful to the low-carbon investor.

Morningstar, for example, using data provided by Sustainalytics, evaluates the degree to which a company's economic value is at risk in the transition to a low-carbon economy _and assigns a carbon-risk rating to each company in a fund._ They are then able to apply an aggregated score to the fund itself.

These are the sorts of technical and informational developments that make it easier for individual investors, institutional investors and professional money managers to transition to low-carbon, fossil-fuel free investing strategies.

Summary

Clearly the sustainable investing industry has made enormous progress in the last five years. Yet much more needs to be done.

There is nothing more deserving of the oft used political phrase "The Fierce Urgency of Now" than the looming danger of unchecked global warming, with all of its devastating follow-on consequences for humanity.

It behooves every one of us to take any and all measures we can — and to go beyond our "comfort zones" — to tackle this profound existential challenge.

Fortunately, when it comes to our personal retirement plans and individual investment accounts, the resources and tools exist to radically decarbonize our investment portfolios, and to do so _without making a financial sacrifice._

I invite you, dear reader, to join me in this critically important effort to align our beliefs with our personal investment practices, while making an important contribution to the global struggle to save our species from the ravages of global warming.

2013 INTRODUCTION

This book explores the concept of "Green" Investing, which has as its key postulate the desire of many investors to direct their investment dollars to businesses that are Socially Responsible, while earning a competitive return.

The first impediment to Green Investing is one of perception. More than a few people are afflicted with the belief that Socially Responsible investors are relegated to a world of sub-par investment performance. They may be admirably following their hearts, the thinking goes, but investors who invest through the prism of social responsibility are nevertheless making a financial sacrifice.

This is demonstrably not the case. Like other instances of faulty conventional wisdom, the canard that Socially Responsible Investing (SRI) inevitably leads to less than optimal investment returns can be quickly dispelled by looking at the facts.

On March 12, 2012, *Morningstar*, a well known company that offers investment information and independent mutual fund analysis (www.Morningstar.com), published an article by David Kathman, a Chartered Financial Analyst, entitled "Social Responsibility and Fund Performance."

After digesting a substantial amount of statistical research (summarized in the article), Mr. Kathman concludes with the following statement: "In essence, these studies have found that social screening is a "free good.""

In other words, after evaluating the data, he determined that there is no absolute performance "cost" to investors for utilizing socially responsible screening techniques when building investment portfolios.

The investor must still follow sound principles when designing a portfolio and selecting investments, but the addition of Socially Responsible screening, in and of itself, has been shown to have a neutral impact on performance.

Indexes represent the average value of baskets of stocks, bonds and other securities. They are useful tools that help us recognize broad market trends in the midst of a forest of data points. Some indexes measure the value of very specific types of investments, like healthcare stocks, or high yield bonds, while others reflect broader groupings, such as large domestic stocks.

As of January 13, 2012, the Calvert Social Responsibility Index (Symbol "CALVIN") of more than 600 Socially Responsible companies had a better five year performance record than does the widely followed Standard and Poor's 500 Index (Symbol "INX") of 500 conventionally selected companies.

Skeptics may "split hairs" dissecting index composition or debating the relevance of index performance over various time periods, but this simple comparison of indices is illuminating. Clearly investors with a socially responsible orientation do not *automatically* face a performance handicap.

I encourage the reader to go to Calvert.com and Standardand Poors.com for more information on the composition of these Indexes.

This Book is a Call to Action!

My goal is to provide you with practical, real world information that will orient you in today's investing environment.

When you have digested the information provided in this book, you will be able to function as a Green investor and confidently add an SRI component to your investment process.

You will also have the information you need to avoid the pitfalls of exorbitant fees, unnecessarily limited investment options, misleading propaganda from Big Brand financial firms, and compromised advice from so-called financial professionals.

This Book Is For You If:

- You're curious about the concept of Green Investing
- You'd like to incorporate SRI principles into your investment process without sacrificing performance
- You're accumulating a nest egg that you'd like to invest for the long term
- You'd like to know more about the scientific principles involved in building a risk-adjusted diversified investment portfolio
- You notice a contrast between the financial media's non-stop coverage of short-term stock price fluctuations, and the relative scarcity of advice about developing a long-term investment strategy
- You're skeptical about investment advice offered by the national banks and brand name financial institutions, many of which nearly self-destructed during the economic collapse of 2008

Once the misapprehensions are gone; and armed with the information and knowledge shared in this book, the educated Green investor will be ready to build a strong, diversified, Sustainable investment portfolio.

Unpacking the Concept of Green Investing

Green Investing, with SRI at its core, encompasses the totality of the individual investing experience.

> *Green Investing, with SRI at its core, encompasses the totality of the individual investing experience.*

The Green investor is an informed consumer who seeks to invest prudently and responsibly; someone who has a basic working knowledge of investment strategy and the broad investing environment. She is prepared to embrace opportunities and navigate past obstacles as she takes ownership of her investing efforts.

For the purposes of this book, Socially Responsible Investing will be defined as the investment-specific core of Green Investing, and it will represent the discrete process of selecting investments for your portfolio that show strong growth potential *and* are compatible with your ethical and moral values.

Green investors will benefit by understanding the principles behind the design of risk-adjusted investment portfolios. Only after an appropriate investment template has been created should the socially responsible investment screening take place.

Successful Green investing requires an understanding of, and familiarity with today's investing landscape. An important feature of this terrain is the ubiquitous sales and marketing presence of the huge national and multi-national financial organizations.

The power implicit in this omnipresence is wielded daily like an enormous magnet, drawing investors and their hard-earned money into the maw of these firms' turbocharged sales operations.

Bolstered by an informed awareness of the tactics and objectives of the Big Brand firms, the investor can immunize herself against their immense marketing power and stay focused on her personal objectives.

Green investors should also be aware that the financial media's obsession with short-term market movements can be a seriously counter-productive influence on anyone striving to build a diversified, risk-adjusted investment portfolio.

Finally, when seeking financial advice, the Green investor should understand the different skill sets and professional obligations of a wide variety of financial professionals including insurance agents, registered representatives, registered investment advisors, wealth managers, financial advisors, and Certified Financial Planners™.

In summary, this book will help aspiring Green investors do the following:

- Understand the meaning and utility of SRI
- Develop a simple, practical approach to SRI that can be applied successfully to their own portfolios
- Demystify the process of creating a high quality, risk adjusted diversified investment portfolio
- Become better informed while navigating an investing environment filled with marketing propaganda from Big Brand financial organizations
- Avoid being misled and exploited by people who hold themselves out as financial professionals
- See past the daily television and internet stream of esoteric financial data points and trader-centric commentary, most of which is of questionable value to the long-term investor

When you, the investor, are in possession of adequate knowledge in these inter-related areas, you will truly be able to function as a *Green* investor. Are you ready for the challenge?

How this Book is Organized
In Chapter 1, I'll provide an overview of Socially Responsible Investing, the core of Green investing.

In Chapter 2, you'll learn how to incorporate SRI screening into your investment strategy while staying focused on investment performance.

In Chapter 3, I'll define common investment vehicles.

In Chapter 4, I'll explain what you need to do *before* implementing the SRI screening process. We'll investigate the art, science and technology involved in building a diversified long-term investment portfolio that is calibrated to your goals and tolerance for risk.

In Chapter 5, we'll take a "big picture" view of today's investing environment, and I'll offer tips to help you:

- Avoid being distracted, confused or mislead by the financial media
- Understand the credentials, titles, and obligations of those who call themselves financial professionals
- Realize that investing through huge national investment firms or banks is not necessarily the best approach for the Green investor

In Chapter 6, I'll summarize the Green investing principles we've explored and provide you with an *Action Plan* you can use to move forward with your own Green approach to successful Socially Responsible Investing.

Don't blow it — good planets are hard to find.

QUOTED IN TIME

CHAPTER 1

The What, How and Why of SRI/ESG

Let's start with the basics. Socially Responsible Investing (SRI) is an approach that seeks to maximize both investment return for the investor *and* social good for the society in which we live. SRI appeals to investors who, while achieving their investment goals, have an interest in using their accumulated savings to enhance the world in ways they themselves choose.

Investors take different approaches to SRI: Some are more concerned about *avoiding* certain industries such as tobacco, alcohol, firearms or gambling.

Others are more concerned about the industries, companies or countries they want to *support*. For example, a particular SRI investor may seek worthwhile investments in the renewable energy industry, or search for competitive multi-national firms that make a concerted effort to ensure fair treatment of suppliers' foreign workers.

Still other SRI investors may pursue a strategy that emphasizes religious values, or favors investments in developing countries that show a strong commitment to democratic institutions and the rule of law.

The good news is that SRI can encompass all of the above. This book will help guide the individual investor as she develops her own socially responsible screening protocol and integrates it into her investing experience.

Socially Responsible Investing Can Make a Difference

Using investment strategies to achieve political, economic or social goals is not new. The most dramatic example of the power of SRI is the disinvestment campaign successfully carried out in protest against the South African government in the 1970s and 1980s.

Participants included university endowment funds, religious leaders, individual corporations, state pension funds, federal politicians, and local municipalities.

Nelson Mandela has stated that the University of California's multibillion dollar divestment was particularly significant in abolishing white minority rule in South Africa.

This history-changing example illustrates how investors, large and small, can positively influence the world by being thoughtful about their investments.

I'm sure most readers will agree that a host of critical problems challenge the world today, every bit as urgently as the anti-apartheid struggle did decades ago.

A comprehensive, Green approach to personal investing, with social responsibility and sustainability at its core, is another tool we can use to address these problems in a nuanced and individualized way.

Skepticism is Natural, but Unfounded

Most of us have simple objectives when it comes to our investments. We want them to make money for us, and we don't want to spend unreasonable amounts of time managing them.

When people first hear about SRI, they may have their doubts. After all, the idea of using investment criteria other than hard-headed personal profit potential is quite new to most of us. Don't we have to put our ethical concerns to the side when considering investment opportunities?

What about the time and extra knowledge required?

Few of us have the time or analytical background needed to research whether a particular multi-national company sources its raw materials in a sustainable way, or ensures that its foreign suppliers honor social justice principles when hiring, managing and compensating their work force.

People unacquainted with SRI may believe that socially responsible investors are somewhat naïve, investing primarily in exotic alternative technologies or whimsical ventures that are unproven and underfunded.

When we distill the concerns and doubts investors have about SRI, we end up with the following core issues:

- Investment Performance
- Time Commitment
- Knowledge Required
- Obscurity of Investments

This book will help investors like you see that SRI *can* deliver competitive performance, does <u>not</u> involve an emphasis on obscure investments, does <u>not</u> require an excessive time commitment and does <u>not</u> depend upon the investor becoming an expert analyst.

In fact, the field of SRI attracts clear-eyed pragmatists, many of whom believe that adding SRI criteria to their investment selection process can help them find profitable businesses poised to thrive as the future unfolds.

Companies that score well based on SRI criteria may have an edge when it comes to cultivating a committed and diversified workforce.

They may also be less likely to experience regulatory and legal challenges in the future. Smaller, fast-growing SRI-based companies may find it easier to raise money from venture capital firms.

In fact, the field of SRI attracts clear-eyed pragmatists, many of whom believe that adding SRI criteria to their investment selection process can help them find profitable businesses, poised to thrive as the future unfolds.

No Need to Reinvent the Wheel

A professional class of Socially Responsible money managers emerged in the early 1970s, and has been evolving steadily for more than 40 years.

These SRI professionals make their research and expertise available to individual investors through investment vehicles such as mutual funds, exchange-traded funds (ETFs) and separate accounts.

In future chapters, we'll discuss these investment vehicles, or tools, in more detail, with a primary focus on mutual funds.

For now, it is important for the reader to know that mutual funds and ETFs are pools of stocks, bonds, and other assets. Their shares are traded daily and easily available to investors.

Leveraging the expertise of professional SRI money managers, this book presents busy investors with an efficient method they can use to effectively apply Socially Responsible screening to their own investment portfolios.

Leveraging the expertise of professional SRI money managers, this book presents busy investors with an efficient method they can use to effectively apply Socially Responsible screening to their own investment portfolios.

Strength in Numbers: Opportunity for Advocacy

SRI investors have had positive impacts on some of the world's largest corporations by banding together under the umbrella of an SRI mutual fund family (Socially responsible ETFs may soon offer a similar opportunity).

These fund families are able to *advocate* for progressive change at individual corporations, using the aggregate wealth of the fund's shareholders as leverage. Fund analysts scrutinize corporate behavior and focus on positive changes that a company could be encouraged to implement, as a way of attracting more SRI investor interest.

Specific suggestions may be made to a company's board of directors, executives and managers. In some cases, external pressure can be applied, in the form of boycotts, petitions or public messages highlighting areas where SRI advocates feel improvements should and can be made.

Corporations with large, visible operations and management structures tend to have the infrastructure necessary to provide rigorous oversight and control of their institutional behaviors.

A large multi-national firm is likely to be quite sensitive about its public image. This may provide additional incentive for corporate managers to respond positively to socially responsible investors. The professional SRI community works closely with some of the largest corporations in the world, both as shareholders and as advocates for positive change. Individual investors, by investing in socially responsible mutual funds, can play an important role in this process. Appendix B, on page 146, contains an explanation by the Calvert fund family of their approach to SRI advocacy.

Abbreviations and Acronyms Abound

As SRI grows in popularity, certain advocates are seeking to change or modify the branding of the community to improve visibility or more accurately identify core objectives.

For example, some believe that the "S" in "SRI" should represent the word "Sustainable" to convey a more defined and unified idea of purpose.

Occasionally new terms replace old ones, sometimes leading to confusion. You may be aware of terms such as "Ethical Investing" or "Conscious Investing", both of which are synonymous with "Socially Responsible Investing."

The abbreviation "CSR" is used by the Haas School of Business at the University of California, Berkeley to represent "Corporate Social Responsibility."

"Impact Investing" has recently become a very popular term — who *doesn't* want to have a positive impact with his investment strategy?

The conceptual strength of the word "impact" has led investment managers of many different stripes to use it in their marketing collateral.

Unfortunately, when it comes to the specifics of Impact Investing, the problem for investors is two-fold:

1 The term "Impact Investing" is vague, does not represent a particular investing methodology, and lacks a meaningful long term track record.
2 It's easy for the average investor to confuse "Impact Investing" with "Socially Responsible Investing" (SRI), or "Green" investing.

In contrast, SRI *does* have a very specific investment methodology, developed carefully over 40 years. SRI focuses on how corporations interact with the *environment,* how management cultures address *social justice* issues such as employee working conditions, and how executive leadership teams *govern* their public enterprises.

Thus the abbreviation "ESG" (representing the Environment, Social Justice and Governance) is frequently used when discussing SRI, to specify the areas of primary concern to SRI fund managers.

It is important to understand that for the purpose of Socially Responsible Investing, fund managers *measure corporate practices in these three areas against those of the companies' peers,* not against an absolute standard of perfection.

The process is not unlike what teachers in high school used to call "grading on a curve."

Why don't SRI fund managers seek out only those corporations that meet a very high standard of excellence in these three (E-S-G) areas? The answer to this question goes to the heart of the difference between Impact Investing (which has no particular investing protocol) and the carefully pragmatic approach known as SRI:

SRI fund managers have as a co-primary goal the attainment of a competitive return for their investors.

By "competitive," I mean that SRI fund managers strive to earn rates of return for their investors equal to or better than those enjoyed by investors who do not use an SRI screening component.

Additionally, it is a well-known fact that for the average investor, diversification is an essential element of prudent investing. SRI investors are no different — they should hold stocks and bonds issued by corporations of different sizes, from different countries and from different industries.

To summarize: While "Impact Investing" clearly means vastly different things to different people, "Green Investing" as defined in this book, follows closely the dual mandate of the Socially Responsible Investing industry:

> *Earn a competitive return while investing in a diverse mix of corporations that have the best ESG scorecards compared to their peers.*

The sudden ubiquity of the term "Impact Investing" may be a challenge to the integrity of the SRI movement — some multi-national firms driving the concept have enormous amounts of money they can deploy to entice investors into an approach that may not be what it appears to be.

The SRI industry must make sure that its brand does not get diluted, the same way that merchants selling truly organic foods must strive to make sure their brand is not diluted by nebulous food label marketing claims like "All Natural."

This type of marketing or branding confusion is exactly *why* I emphasize the comprehensive approach described as Green Investing. Green investors will look beyond the name or brand of an SRI, ESG or Impact fund to discern its managers' investment priorities and assess the integrity and core values of the people behind it.

So by all means, if you are a philanthropist, consider working with a trusted and qualified advisor to devise an investment strategy that will have an impact in an area of importance to you.

Don't worry about an immediate return, or even an eventual return on your investment — your goal is to have an impact.

I am not being sarcastic; I know and respect people who run progressive, environmentally friendly Impact investing programs.

However, if you are like most investors, you need to earn a competitive return on your investments.

Most of us cannot afford the luxury of only investing in a few "super-green" companies, or limiting our investments to a couple of worthwhile industries.

Green investing strategies using SRI funds will allow you to pragmatically pursue your investing goals while nudging the corporate world toward a better, greener future.

Scrutinizing Corporations through the SRI Lens

Below are listed several examples of positive corporate behaviors SRI investors might look for:

- Companies that emphasize recycling and energy efficiency in their internal operations
- Companies protecting critical natural resources such as rainforests, biodiversity, clean air and water
- Companies careful not to exploit workforces in other countries (which may have minimal labor protection laws)

- Companies that demonstrate internal hiring and promotional practices that are gender, race, religion and sexual orientation neutral
- Companies displaying transparency and accountability with respect to internal governance and management practices, while maintaining independent and attentive Boards of Directors

It's important to realize that although the various members of the SRI community share basic principles, particularly the dual mandate of competitive return and comparatively strong ESG scorecards, there is still a healthy diversity within the industry.

Individual investors, SRI mutual fund families and other managers of capital with SRI investment objectives each have their own criteria, priorities and methodologies for selecting securities.

Such diversity allows individual investors to sort through a number of SRI asset managers and align themselves with those whose screening priorities best match their own.

What's the Current State of the SRI Universe?

As of November 2012, the Social Investment Forum reports that total U.S. SRI assets have grown 22 per cent in two years to a total of $3.74 trillion.

This represents about 10% of the American investment marketplace.

The June, 2012 issue of *Kiplinger's* says that there are now 493 SRI mutual funds, with aggregate current value of $569 billion. In 1995, there were only 55 SRI funds, with total assets of $12 billion. That's pretty rapid growth over a 17 year period.

In addition to individuals, SRI investors include religious institutions, corporations, universities, pension funds, and other entities that wish to invest based on varied sets of social, ethical, governance and environmental criteria. Institutional investors currently represent the fastest growing and largest source of investment dollars in the SRI universe.

Acknowledging the Success of SRI

During the last few years there has been a crescendo of academic research and real world validation underscoring the success of Socially Responsible Investing concepts.

This proof of concept is very meaningful — not just for investors, but also for money managers and analysts seeking new sets of criteria useful in the search for companies likely to thrive in future.

Finance programs at universities, geared to teaching students how and why ethics are an important element in successful business strategies, are in demand.

It's worth mentioning again that in March of 2012, Morningstar published a research article by Chartered Financial Analyst David Kathman in which, after reviewing substantial data, he concluded that social screening is a "free good."

In the May, 2012 issue of Kiplinger's magazine, James Glassman wrote a column called "Do-Gooders Do Better." In his opening sentence, he states that "In the world of investing, conscience, it seems, costs nothing."

He then cites as evidence comparisons between widely followed unscreened indexes (including the S&P 500) and both a sustainably screened index, the ESG MSCi USA Select Index (Symbol KLD), and a comparable Calvert mutual fund.

In June of 2012, a 72-page report from DB Climate Change Advisors, a unit of Deutsche Bank Group, looked at more than 100 academic studies and 56 research papers, with the goal of understanding whether sustainable investing (SRI) contributes to long-term value and performance.

Managing director Mark Fulton summarized their findings by declaring, "We believe that ESG (environmental, social and governance) analysis should be built in(to) the investment processes of every serious investor…ESG best-in-class focused funds should be able to capture superior risk-adjusted returns if well executed."

Catching the Attention of the Big Brand Financial Firms

The June, 2012 issue of Financial Advisor magazine contains two articles addressing what could be called the "mainstreaming" of SRI concepts.

In "Class Act," the author states that academic research has linked environmental, social and governance factors with strong investment returns. Driven by this evidence, universities around the globe have begun to infuse sustainable and responsible investing, and corporate social responsibility principles and practices into their curricula.

In the article, a lecturer at the Hass School of Business at the University of California at Berkeley talks about an MBA course he offers called "Social Investing: Recent Findings in Management and Finance." He also references an SRI money management firm for which he is chief investment officer. The firm is owned by Wells Fargo bank.

The second article in the June, 2012 issue of Financial Advisor, entitled "The New, Bold Face of Impact Investing" features an interview with a J. P. Morgan money manager who is expanding into an investment methodology he calls "Impact Investing." This Wall Street firm veteran is clearly eager to exploit what industry insiders say is a growing trend among wealthy individuals: seeking to invest with an eye toward more than just personal gain.

The concept of Impact Investing resonates with people interested in SRI because of a shared theme: Investing can accomplish more than simply increasing one's personal wealth.

However, as discussed earlier on pages 13 through 15, Impact Investing goals vary widely based on the objectives of each investor, and may not address the environment, social justice or corporate governance at all.

It's important that investors with SRI objectives do not conflate Impact Investing with Green or Socially Responsible Investing.

SRI Does Not Require Financial Sacrifice

What can an investor interested in Socially Responsible Investing learn from these news reports, investing trends and academic studies? The fundamental message is that contrary to what some may believe, SRI does not automatically require financial sacrifice.

This is my key thesis — not that SRI is superior to conventional investing, but that it is not inferior.

This is my key thesis — not that SRI is superior to conventional investing, but that it is not *inferior*.

Some specialized asset classes such as Emerging Markets stock may not yet be readily accessible through a diverse number of SRI ETFs or mutual funds. For this reason, SRI investors seeking broad diversification may choose to use non-SRI mutual funds or individual equities for a portion of their portfolios.

However, when it comes to the core asset classes, the data show that mutual funds and exchange-traded funds incorporating an SRI screening process can deliver performance comparable, and in some cases superior to that generated by non-SRI based conventionally managed funds.

The Non-SRI Elements of Green Investing

Size Does Matter

The rest of this Chapter is an introduction and prelude to the more detailed discussion of Big Brand financial firms included in Chapter 5.

As mentioned earlier, the term "Green Investing" is used to broaden the discussion of SRI beyond simply the investment methodology. We as investors need to be prepared for the other peripheral aspects of the personal investing process: To whom should we go for financial advice? What sort of financial professional can deliver the best customer experience?

How do we stay focused on our need for objective financial advice and information while being bombarded with the incessant marketing efforts of the huge financial firms?

Without naming names, it might be useful for investors to review some of the more recent enforcement actions taken, and allegations leveled against national banks and major Wall Street corporations. In the past couple of years, several of these firms have paid eight and nine-figure fines to settle a variety of charges, including predatory lending, bid-rigging and discrimination against borrowers of color.

Financial Advisors employed by one well-known Wall Street brokerage house have accused management of systematically pressuring the sales force to sell the firm's proprietary products over competitor's investments also offered by the firm. At the same time, this firm was touting the presence of non-proprietary investments as evidence that their representatives offered objective financial advice.

As investors, this story and other similar ones beg the question: Do we want to pay Wall Street firms and national banks for the "privilege" of using their systems to access their version of socially responsible investing?

If you are interested in SRI, it makes sense to look first to independent Financial Planners, particularly those who can offer access to a wide variety of SRI-focused mutual funds and exchange-traded funds.

When building your portfolio, try to choose funds that have been committed to SRI for years, and can show strong long-term track records.

There are now a number of large regional firms offering Financial Planning and money management services to the public.

Although these firms may not be directly controlled by the mammoth Wall Street firms, their size may create certain risks and limitations for their clients.

One reason size can be problematic is the obvious — there is a point at which a firm is so large, individual investors lack significance.

You, as the client or investor, are easily replaced with another client and not terribly missed if you choose to leave.

When you work with a smaller firm, you represent a more substantial portion of the firm's business, and you are likely to receive more personalized service. This, of course, is not guaranteed, but your odds are better with a small firm.

The other reasons to be leery of large firms are more subtle. Over time, if the "corporate mentality" takes hold, the personal touch may erode.

Inevitably large firms have more layers of employees, and with multiple offices and people seeking internal promotion you may lose connection with the person with whom you formed the initial relationship.

A regional financial services company may consider going public, focusing ever more on the short-term bottom line to attract investors and satisfy the demands of investment bankers and potential shareholders.

Picayune cost cutting measures may be implemented, even though the client experience is negatively impacted.

As firms grow large, decision-makers may look for ways to capture more revenue per client. What's an easy way to do that? One way is for the firm to launch its own funds, or other investment products.

These firms then can potentially get paid twice by their clients — once for Financial Planning services that include the creation of an investment strategy, and then again as the managers or originators of the firm's proprietary investments.

Conflicts of Interest, Titles, Checks and Balances

One of the biggest challenges for the SRI investor seeking financial advice is finding a financial professional whose advice is not tainted by undisclosed conflicts of interest.

Conflicts of interest can be as innocuous as offering clients a limited roster of funds or investment products.

Clients may be told that limiting their choices saves them from being overwhelmed, but too often these limits serve the financial purposes of the firm or advisor.

Investors interested in SRI should query financial professionals directly — ask them to explain any conflicts of interest, and whether the system they use offers clients access to a full range of SRI mutual fund families.

Unfortunately, the financial services industry is awash with confusing titles — Financial Consultant, Financial Advisor, Wealth Manager and Financial Planner are several of the most common.

Some of us have letters after our names, potentially signifying additional training, but typically incomprehensible to the general public.

A Certified Financial Planner™ is required by the Certified Financial Planner Board of Standards to act as the client's fiduciary, the same standard of care required from attorneys.

Among other things, the fiduciary standard means that a CFP® must accept an obligation to always put clients' interests first, and to provide full disclosure of conflicts of interest.

Even if you meet a person holding herself out as a CFP®, it is wise to ask questions about potential conflicts of interest, and make other prudent inquiries to assure yourself that this person can provide you with the quality of service you deserve.

Chapter 5 contains more detail about titles and designations.

Separation of function is a very important concept. Investors stand a better chance of avoiding conflicts of interest when financial advice, fund management and fund-rating analysis are each provided by a different, unrelated entity.

The financial professional offering advice can play the role of strategist and advisor, providing a pathway to investments managed by fund managers who are independent of the financial professional's firm.

You and your financial professional can choose funds for your portfolio based upon fund-rating information provided by an outside consulting firm, such as Morningstar, or Value Line.

This separation of function strategy protects you from the possibility that the financial advisor's firm's internal fund-rating system favors its own investment products, or those of companies with which the firm has a favored relationship.

Besides avoiding conflicts of interest, separation of function in Financial Planning is important for safety's sake.

It is safer for the investor if the financial professional's firm only serves as a conduit for your assets — not a repository.

> *Separation of function is very important — investors benefit when financial advice, fund management and fund-rating analysis are each provided by a different, unrelated entity.*

Mid-sized regional firms may hold client funds and assets for some period of time before the assets reach an outside clearinghouse. This procedure carries some risk.

If an executive at such a firm decides to do something illegal with client money, or the firm makes a disastrous investment decision and comingles investor assets with firm assets, it may be difficult for investors to recover money that was stuck within the firm's coffers at the wrong time.

Investors need checks and balances. If you are using a financial professional to access the securities markets, make sure you have real-time online access to a record of all account trading activity.

Major clearinghouses have websites for this purpose. Investors should periodically verify the accuracy of monthly statements by comparing the reports they receive to information provided through the online database.

Two Sides (or more) to Every Story

Although I have been very clear about my preferences, it is possible that a large firm could provide some clients with a special service or product that would be difficult for a small firm or independent consultant to deliver.

Some investors have special needs, and I don't pretend to know exactly what every large organization offers. I do know that complicated products can be very difficult for investors to fully understand, and that without a solid knowledge of how a product works, investors may misjudge the riskiness of including such a product in their portfolios.

I do feel that based on the criteria I consider most important, smaller local financial firms or consultancies that specialize in SRI are likely to be a better choice for investors seeking a high quality Green investing experience.

I think the environment should be put in the category of our national security. Defense of our resources is just as important as defense abroad. Otherwise what is there to defend?

ROBERT REDFORD, YOSEMITE NATIONAL PARK DEDICATION, 1985

CHAPTER 2

Using SRI/ESG Concepts

How can busy people with an average level of investment expertise avoid supporting industries, countries and corporate management practices that run counter to their personal values?

As investors, how can we select companies we'd like to support? And how can all of this be done within the framework of prudent long-term investing?

As investors, how can we select companies we'd like to support? And how can all of this be done within the framework of prudent long-term investing, which must take into account an individual's risk tolerance, as well as key values such as diversification, need for liquidity, tax impacts, time horizon and more?

Answers to these questions can be framed by the reality that investors and their Financial Planners do not have to start from scratch. The goals cited above can be attained by first using current technology to develop a sound investment portfolio template, and then augmenting this template with the methodical application of a Socially Responsible Investing (SRI) screening process that builds on the accumulated knowledge, research and labor of successful SRI fund managers.

Mutual Funds Play an Important Role

Like many investors, you probably lead a busy life and wonder if you have the time or expertise to incorporate SRI into your investment strategy. That's why I recommend creating an investment portfolio made up of mutual funds and/or exchange-traded funds (ETFs) that use SRI criteria congruent with your personal objectives.

Risk Disclosures

Investments in stocks, bonds, mutual funds and exchange traded funds are subject to market risk, including the possible loss of principal invested. Investors should carefully consider their investment objectives, their risk tolerance and the individual risk/reward attributes of any fund, individual stock or bond instrument considered for investment.

Additionally, before investing in a fund, investors should read the fund prospectus carefully and make sure they understand the risks and objectives of the fund, as well as the internal fund costs and potential transaction costs when buying or selling shares of the fund. Fund prospectuses are available online from the fund company offering the fund, or by mail if requested.

Always remember that an investor's shares, once redeemed, may be worth more or less than the original cost, and that current fund performance may be lower or higher than shown in historical performance data.

Diversification

Diversification, while important and useful as a way to manage risk in a portfolio, does not eliminate risk, does not assure a profit, and does not guarantee against loss in a declining market.

WHAT IS A MUTUAL FUND? I provide an in-depth explanation of mutual funds and other common investment vehicles in Chapter 3. For now, what you need to know is that a mutual fund is a pool or basket of numerous stocks, bonds and other securities. A fund issues shares, and when you own a share of a fund, you own a small portion of each of the assets held by the fund.

Mutual funds and their ETF cousins are efficient tools for portfolio construction. A purchase or sale of a few fund shares means adding or eliminating exposure to a substantial number of individual securities.

You, the investor, can achieve significant diversification by holding a portfolio of five to 10 mutual funds and/or ETFs, and if necessary you can make portfolio changes quickly. If you purchase actively managed funds, your portfolio may benefit from the expertise of the professional money managers running the funds.

Mutual fund shares are bought from, or sold to the fund — generally on a daily basis, providing excellent liquidity (ease of conversion to and from cash) to the investing public. Funds are categorized to indicate the types of assets they hold, and there is ample fund rating information published by companies such as *Morningstar, Value Line* and others to help you compare the track records and compositions of funds to one another.

You can find fund ratings information at *Morningstar.com* or on internet sites such as *Google* and *Yahoo Finance*. If you seek more in-depth fund information, *Morningstar, Lipper* and other services publish detailed analyst reports, explaining their rationale for the ratings they assign to each fund.

Much of this information is now also available for ETFs, although their track records are generally shorter than those of established mutual funds.

Remember to always assess the objectivity of organizations that rate mutual funds and ETFs. Mutual fund ratings, analyst reports or recommendations issued by organizations that also create or manage their *own* funds should be evaluated carefully with an eye to potential conflicts of interest.

The lay investor should also pay attention to ratings methodology: Does the fund rating organization incorporate historical volatility as well as performance into the rating system? If so, how much weight is assigned to volatility, compared to performance?

It is also important to remember that although a fund may be rated highly for past performance/volatility, this fact does not guarantee that it will continue to perform as well in the future.

An experienced Financial Planner can help you evaluate and monitor the quality of mutual funds and ETFs. It is important to look beyond the ratings that are assigned to them to determine if they are suitable for you within the context of your personal investment strategy.

A fund's focus and risk/reward profile can evolve over time, and its purpose in your portfolio should be re-evaluated periodically. You can learn more about SRI funds by browsing fund family websites and other SRI related internet sites, or by reading financial publications that aggregate SRI fund information.

How Are Investment Portfolios Designed?

In Chapter 4, I provide a more in-depth explanation of Portfolio Optimization, the art and science of designing an investment portfolio. The overarching goal is to match the investor's risk tolerance and circumstances with an optimum combination of stocks, bonds and other assets.

For now it's important to know that a thorough job of portfolio construction requires the use of fact-finders, questionnaires, Portfolio Optimization software, and current financial markets data. The data analysis and software tools are best utilized and applied with the help of a Financial Planner. She can help you understand the relevance of the information to your own unique circumstances.

The fact-finding process takes into account your financial circumstances, time horizon, emotional makeup, and investment experience. A questionnaire is used to assess your risk tolerance. A sample Risk Tolerance Questionnaire is included at the end of this book as Appendix C.

The fact finding and risk tolerance data is entered into the Portfolio Optimization software, which in turn generates a *portfolio template*.

This template specifies the percentage of the portfolio that should be allocated to each type or class of asset. By "asset class" I mean investment categories such as large domestic value stocks, small foreign growth stocks, US Treasury bonds or high yield corporate bonds (to name a few).

The portfolio template *does not* specify exactly which funds should be purchased. It only describes how much of the portfolio should be allocated to each *type* of asset class. Only after this part of the process is complete do you begin choosing specific SRI investments.

Creating a Personalized SRI Screen

Many investors interested in SRI will be content to populate their template with quality funds defined by the fund managers as Socially Responsible.

Others may want to dig deeper into the specific screening criteria used by each fund manager, and work a little harder to find the SRI funds with screening priorities that best match their own ethical preferences.

One way to do this is to create a personalized SRI "screen." This will allow you to develop and implement an SRI strategy that applies your values and philosophy to the investment selection process.

The investor who wishes to probe more deeply into the screening process will review the systems used by SRI fund families of interest and select those funds whose processes align best with their own preferences.

Examples of mutual fund screening systems can be found in Appendices A and B at the end of this book.

Your SRI screen will serve as a statement of the investment criteria you will use during the creation of your investment portfolio.

Which corporate behaviors are most important to you, and what sorts of corporations (or governments) do you want to include or exclude? Your screen should state and prioritize your SRI objectives.

How to Apply Your SRI Screen

If you decide to create a personal SRI screen, you will be able to use it as a frame of reference when selecting specific funds representing the asset classes specified by your portfolio template.

This screening process involves identifying SRI mutual funds or ETFs that *include* or *exclude* stocks and bonds based on criteria that match up well with the priorities and values you identify through the creation of your SRI screen.

If several good quality funds representing the same asset class are available, you have the luxury of selecting the fund that is using screening criteria aligned best with your SRI priorities and goals.

If you are working with a Financial Planner who uses an "open architecture" approach ("open architecture" refers to a system that does not limit the investor to a certain group of mutual funds), you will be able to review the track records and ratings histories of a multitude of SRI funds run by different fund companies.

This is important, because one SRI fund family may have a highly-rated fund in one asset class, while another family has a better rating for its fund in a different asset class.

No one fund family has a monopoly on all asset classes, and the best portfolio requires diversity and quality in its holdings.

Each SRI fund family will have its own analytic process and specific screening methodology. One fund family may cater to a particular set of religious sensibilities, while another describes its primary SRI mission as supporting social and economic justice.

This variation in approach by fund family may help you "fine tune" your portfolio using funds that match *your* SRI priorities as closely as possible.

Purchasing Assets

Now that you have applied your screening process to select highly-rated funds that match your SRI criteria, it's time to implement the investment plan and purchase the quantity and types of funds (or in some cases, individual securities) specified by the portfolio template.

For example, if you have a $1 million dollar portfolio, and the template calls for 20 percent of the portfolio to be invested in large cap domestic growth stocks, you'll invest $200,000 of the portfolio in the large cap domestic funds that best satisfy your SRI screening criteria.

In some instances, the timing of purchases can be very important. You will need to decide whether purchases should be made all at once or systematically over time. Periodic investments over time can mitigate certain risks.

What Role Does the Financial Planner Play?

An SRI Financial Planner should first be able to develop a diversified portfolio template for you that is appropriate to your financial circumstances, risk tolerance, time horizon and investment experience.

Access to a wide variety of fund families gives you the best chance of finding the management quality and asset class diversification you'll need when building a strong SRI-based portfolio.

VERY IMPORTANT: She must also be able to provide access to a significant number of Socially Responsible funds and fund families.

This can be a challenge, because many financial professionals operate within a system that either limits their (and their clients') access to SRI fund families, limits their ability to customize the investor's portfolio, or both.

Access to a wide variety of fund families gives you the best chance of finding the management quality and asset class diversification you'll need when building a strong SRI-based portfolio.

Your Financial Planner should have an effective process for sorting through, comparing and selecting the top performing SRI mutual fund managers, monitoring SRI fund performance, and regularly rebalancing or replacing funds as necessary.

If you decide to create your own SRI screen, your Financial Planner should also have a system for organizing and prioritizing your personal SRI screening criteria so that together you can match your priorities with those fund families that have similar investment objectives.

Investors can track and compare long-term mutual fund performance, and monitor fund manager activity by using resources available from independent third party organizations such as *Morningstar*, *Value Line* or other independent fund rating services.

What Your SRI Financial Planner *Shouldn't* Do

I do not recommend having a Financial Planner pick the individual stocks and bonds on your behalf.

In my experience, individual stock or bond selection is a difficult job best left to the experts with documented successful track records who have been managing mutual funds, ETFs or other large pools of money for a long time.

Building an SRI Portfolio *without* Using Mutual Funds

If you're an intrepid investor and wish to avoid funds because you'd rather pick individual stocks and bonds yourself, you have your work cut out for you.

You should be prepared to make many transactions; as many as a hundred individual stocks and bonds may be needed to achieve a decent level of diversification.

As you periodically adjust or rebalance the portfolio, additional transactions must be made, the timing of which can have a substantial effect on the performance of your portfolio.

My experience is that very few non-professional investors will enjoy success selecting individual stocks and bonds for their own account.

Separate Accounts

SRI investors with larger accounts also have another option: using institutional money managers who offer something called Separate Accounts (SAs).

These investment firms have in-house analysts and traders who will create a personal fund of various securities for each investor.

There are a small but growing number of Socially Responsible institutional money managers available to investors with larger amounts of money to invest. Chapter 3 contains additional information on SAs.

Real World Compromises

The biggest challenge for investors who wish to work exclusively with SRI funds is diversification. Diversification, when done well, can reduce risk and volatility while minimizing constraints on long-term performance.

Assets classes such as emerging market stocks, commodities or foreign government bonds may lack a sufficient number of quality SRI fund offerings.

One solution to this dilemma is to use non-SRI funds to invest in these categories until the SRI industry expands to include highly-rated funds representing the full range of asset classes.

No Need for an All or Nothing Approach

If SRI appeals to you, but you would rather enter it gradually, consider starting with a modest portion of your total portfolio.

The remainder of your portfolio can be invested conventionally while you gain experience with the SRI investment process.

Summary of the SRI Investment Process

1 Assess your risk tolerance factors, time horizon and investment goals, and create a diversified portfolio template specifying the percentage of your nest egg that will be allocated to each type of asset class.

2 Develop a written description of your personal SRI priorities, preferences and concerns. How specific do you want to be? If you accept a general definition of social responsibility, you may have more options.

3 Identify your preferred SRI fund families: those that use screening criteria most compatible with your SRI objectives.

4 Select top rated SRI funds from your preferred fund families to populate your template. If you have gaps, you can: a) relax your fund rating requirements and consider funds with lower ratings, b) widen your roster of preferred fund families to include those whose SRI screens don't match your own quite as well, or c) select non-SRI funds for the unfilled spots in your template.

5 Choose the mutual funds you will use to populate your portfolio template and determine the best way to access the securities market. Make your purchases.

6 Develop a schedule for monitoring and periodically reviewing the portfolio. If you are working with a Financial Planner, make sure to notify him when personal circumstances or your risk tolerance factors change.

Resources for the SRI Investor

You'll find samples of SRI fund family security selection criteria in Appendix A, starting on page 138 of this book.

SRI Websites

You can learn about SRI basics by searching the Internet for websites sponsored by SRI fund families such as Parnassus and Calvert, or other sites that aggregate industry information. Two interesting and informative SRI aggregator websites are SocialFunds.com and SocialInvest.org.

SOCIALFUNDS.COM is a comprehensive site offering information on the status of current SRI related legislation, performance data on individual SRI funds, and general advice about financial planning.

SOCIALINVEST.ORG is the official website for The Social Investment Forum, a membership association representing firms, institutions and organizations engaged in SRI. As advocates for the SRI industry, The Social Investment Forum is dedicated to advancing the practice and growth of SRI by increasing its visibility, credibility and impact.

I would feel more optimistic about a bright future for man if he spent less time proving that he can outwit Nature and more time tasting her sweetness and respecting her seniority.

ELWYN BROOKS WHITE, ESSAYS OF E.B. WHITE, 1977

CHAPTER 3

Popular Investment Vehicles

In this section of the book I may over-simplify certain investment characteristics for the sake of clarity. Additionally, more obscure investment vehicles and trading strategies may be left out of the conversation entirely.

My goal is to help you understand the *basic* tools available to investors, as well as how to use these tools effectively when building a solid SRI-oriented investment portfolio.

The easiest way to leverage the research and experience of professional SRI investors is to use mutual funds and ETFs. Using these professionally managed baskets of stocks, bonds and other types of assets, an investor avoids the need to do exhaustive research of his own into the SRI-related behaviors of individual corporations.

Risk Disclosures
Investments in stocks, bonds, mutual funds and exchange traded funds are subject to market risk, including the possible loss of principal invested. Investors should carefully consider their investment objectives, their risk tolerance and the individual risk/reward attributes of any fund, individual stock or bond instrument considered for investment.

Additionally, before investing in a fund, investors should read the fund prospectus carefully and make sure they understand the risks and objectives of the fund, as well as the internal fund costs and potential transaction costs when buying or selling shares of the fund. Fund prospectuses are available online from the fund company offering the fund, or by mail if requested.

Always remember that an investor's shares, once redeemed, may be worth more or less than the original cost, and that current fund performance may be lower or higher than shown in historical performance data.

Diversification

Diversification, while important and useful as a way to manage risk in a portfolio, does not eliminate risk, does not assure a profit, and does not guarantee against loss in a declining market.

Mutual Funds in More Depth

Metaphorically speaking, a mutual fund resembles a pie. Pies include a number of ingredients such as sugar, salt, water, spices, and pumpkin. If the filling is mixed properly, each slice should contain the same relative amount of ingredients as any other slice.

If a tiny sliver of the pie is 60 percent pumpkin, 5 percent spice, and 10 percent sugar, a huge slice should have exactly the same percentage of those ingredients.

The *quantity* of each ingredient will vary by size of slice, but not the relative percentage of ingredients. (Feel free to adjust my example to reflect your personal pie preference.)

Similarly, each mutual fund is also a pool of ingredients, typically stocks, bonds and cash. Let's say you have a fund called Home Run, and it holds 75 different types of stocks and bonds.

Each "share" of the fund (don't be confused by terminology; a share of a fund is very different from a share of a stock) is like a slice of the pie; it includes the same proportion of the fund's holdings as every other share. If 5 percent of Home Run is invested in Apple Inc. stock, every share of the fund also contains 5 percent Apple stock.

No matter how many shares of the Home Run fund an investor owns, the comparative ratios of the fund's holdings stay the same — i.e. 5 percent invested in Apple stock.

Shares of most mutual funds can be bought and sold each trading day. The exact price (value) of mutual fund shares is not determined until after the markets close.

This is important to understand — no matter when you decide to buy or sell shares of a mutual fund, the transaction will not occur until after markets close and the value of the fund's holdings has been calculated.

Individual stocks and bonds trade differently — they are bought or sold at specific times during the trading day.

Mutual funds with managers who use their analytic and trading expertise to optimize fund performance are called "actively managed". Organizations such as *Morningstar* and *Value Line* will evaluate and rate these funds by comparing them to each other and to unmanaged market benchmarks. Fund ratings take volatility into account as well as performance.

A fund with lower volatility is preferred by a rational investor if its performance over various time periods is similar to that of a more volatile fund.

Mutual fund "families" are groups of funds with related management that are organized under the same corporate structure. Well known fund families like *Fidelity*, *Oppenheimer* or *American Funds* offer numerous funds, with many different asset types and security selection strategies represented.

Other fund families are much smaller and more specialized. Some

Investors benefit from the fact that an abundance of information is readily available on mutual funds, including their holdings, their managers and their track records.

fund families strive to be "one-stop shops," offering as many kinds of funds as possible. Others are smaller and may focus on achieving excellence in a particular category.

Most mutual fund shares are highly liquid. This means they can be purchased or redeemed from the fund on any business day, as long as the transaction is initiated before the market closes.

Investors benefit from the fact that an abundance of information is readily available on mutual funds, including their holdings, their managers and their track records.

What Are Index Funds?

Index Funds are a subset of mutual funds. They differ from actively managed funds in that they do not rely on stock or bond-picking expertise when selecting their holdings.

Index fund managers choose securities that represent a set of objective quantitative criteria like size, type, region of origin, or industry sector.

Some index mutual funds are constructed to closely track market indexes such as the Dow Jones Industrial Average, the Standard & Poor's 500 Index, or the Nasdaq 100. Other index funds track the average performance of a segment of the economy, such as large domestic growth stocks, short-term U.S. government bonds or pharmaceutical stocks.

Because there are no value judgments being made by fund managers, index funds require little buying and selling of their underlying holdings. The securities held by the fund are meant to simply represent a certain segment of the investment marketplace.

For this reason, they're called "passive" mutual funds. Managing an index fund does not require hiring highly skilled analysts to make opportunistic buying and selling decisions. Consequently, the internal management expenses of index mutual funds can be kept relatively low.

Mutual Fund Investing Philosophies: Active vs. Passive

Some fund families and financial commentators advocate using index funds or passive investing *exclusively*, based on research that shows a relatively small percentage of actively managed funds consistently outperforming their passively managed index fund peers.

Other investment professionals point out that although a minority of actively managed funds consistently outperforms the unmanaged indexes, this minority is still a substantial number of funds.

For example, if only 5 percent of the more than 10,000 mutual funds currently available represent actively managed funds that consistently outperform their passively managed index fund peers, this still equates to more than 500 different mutual funds.

If an investor can develop a successful system for identifying these best-of-breed actively managed funds, it makes sense to invest in them.

Other investment pros aim to combine the advantages of both passive and active investing. Advocates of this approach allocate a portion of the portfolio to active funds in sectors where historical research indicates they are more likely to outperform, while the remainder of the portfolio is allocated to low-expense passive, or index funds.

When you invest in mutual funds, make sure you know what class of shares you are buying, and whether it is the least expensive share class for which you qualify.

There are an increasing number of Index mutual funds based on SRI indexes that can be used to achieve the SRI objective using passive investment principles.

Share Classes of Mutual Funds

The proliferation of different share classes makes it challenging for mutual fund investors to know precisely how, and how much they are paying when they buy shares of a fund.

Some mutual funds deduct a portion of your investment, used to pay a commission, as soon as you purchase the funds — we call those "loaded" funds. So-called "no-load" funds do not charge an initial commission, but may have higher annual costs deducted from the fund than do loaded funds. You can find the details of the fund cost structure in a document called the fund prospectus.

When you invest in mutual funds, make sure you know what class of shares you are buying, and whether it is the least expensive share class for which you qualify.

Always ask if there is a no-load or load-waived share class available — maybe from a different fund company offering a similar type of fund.

Despite the caveats cited above, I believe mutual funds offer an excellent way for an investor to build a diverse portfolio at a reasonable cost while benefiting from professional management, transparency, liquidity and a wide selection of investment categories and methodologies.

ETFs

ETFs, or Exchange Traded Funds, are similar to mutual funds in that their value is tied to the aggregate worth of a pool of underlying assets, or to a market index representing an unmanaged basket of certain categories of stocks, bonds or other assets.

ETFs are also very different from mutual funds because they can be traded immediately when markets are open. Mutual funds are traded at the end of the day after the markets have closed. A shorthand way of describing ETFs is to say that they are similar to mutual funds in terms of diversification, but can be bought or sold immediately during trading hours like individual stocks.

With ETFs, investors can use trading strategies not available to owners of mutual funds, such as stop losses and short selling. Additionally, margin accounts can be opened to leverage the purchase of ETFs with a loan from the brokerage firm.

Most ETFs were initially designed as "passive" investments, similar to index mutual funds. Passive index mutual funds and passive ETFs keep internal expenses low because they do not use a team of experts to decide which securities to buy or sell.

Recently, a flood of different types of *actively* managed ETFs has swept into the marketplace, and these ETFs can be expected to have higher internal fees than their passive brethren.

Some traders are wary of ETFs because their actual linkage to the underlying investments or indexes is highly complex. Because of this, ETF owners can experience substantial "tracking error". This means that the investor can end up with a different return than that of the basket of securities the ETF is supposedly tracking. In some cases, the ETF's name, or stated objective may not clearly correlate to its actual performance.

Also, there are often transaction costs each time an ETF is bought or sold. By comparison, there are numerous ways to trade mutual funds while paying minimal or no transaction fees.

To their advantage, ETFs as a group have lower internal "expense ratios" than most mutual funds, and this may offset the higher transaction costs for certain investors. Another challenge faced by investors considering ETFs is that in most cases they have not been around long enough to establish long-term track records.

There is no question that the positive attributes of ETFs guarantee their survival as a popular investment vehicle. However, their less desirable qualities can make it more difficult to calibrate portfolio diversification or assess relative quality when comparing them to each other or to mutual funds.

There are a number of ETFs currently available that are targeted to the SRI investor, and inevitably others will emerge as interest in Socially Responsible Investing continues to grow.

What is a "Separate Account"?

Think of a Separate Account (SA) as something like a personal mutual fund, managed by institutional money managers who purchase and sell assets for the SA on behalf of a specific investor.

Unlike mutual funds and ETFs, which pool assets and sell shares of the pool to many different investors, each Separate Account is created specifically for a particular owner. Thus there are no *shares* of SAs — the account owner directly owns each of the individual stocks, bonds and other assets held in the account.

Retirement accounts such as IRAs and 401(k) accounts are protected from tax consequences when securities are bought and sold within the accounts (before the investor makes withdrawals).

Managing taxable, non-retirement accounts is a different story, and SAs can offer significant tax advantages when doing so. Each time a stock or bond is sold in this type of account there will be a potential tax consequence (a gain or a loss) that must be accounted for on the current year's tax return. Additionally, stock dividends and bond interest payments received by the investor in after-tax accounts can be taxable.

Because of the control an investor has over when each security is bought and sold within a Separate Account, investors can manage their gains and losses more easily using SAs than they can with mutual funds or ETFs.

To reduce taxes for the year, an investor with an after-tax SA can sell certain securities near year-end that have lost value. This realized loss can then be used to offset capital gains taxes due on other securities that were sold for a profit.

Making changes to Separate Accounts can be labor and paperwork intensive. This is in contrast to mutual funds and ETFs, shares of which can be purchased or sold in a single transaction, allowing investors to quickly add or eliminate exposure to all the stocks and bonds held by that fund.

There is less third-party information available about SAs than there is for mutual funds and ETFs.

Assessing SA quality is a realm where the right Financial Planner could provide valuable assistance to the novice investor.

SRI oriented investors using SAs currently face the following challenges:

- High minimums (typically $100,000 per account holder)
- A limited number of SRI Separate Account managers
- Less asset class diversity among SRI Separate Account managers
- A scarcity of long-term SRI Separate Account performance track records
- A comparatively complicated process when building, modifying or liquidating personal portfolios

SAs are most suitable for investors with at least $500,000 in investible after-tax assets. Given the minimum account size of $100,000 mandated by most SAs, $500,000 could be diversified over at least five different asset classes, providing an acceptable degree of diversification. In the future, I'm sure we'll see more Separate Account managers specializing in SRI.

Alternative Investment Vehicles

Investment vehicles such as options and futures contracts, synthetic derivatives, hedge funds, private equity, alternative investments and Real Estate Investment Trusts are considered alternative investments, and are primarily utilized by sophisticated investors.

In some cases some exposure to alternative investments can help increase portfolio diversification. You may be able to find mutual funds or ETFs that can provide exposure to these alternative asset classes.

CHAPTER 4

Building Strong Investment Portfolios

B efore applying a Socially Responsible Investing (SRI) screening process to your investment process, consider working with a Financial Planner to develop a template for a diversified, risk-adjusted investment portfolio. In this chapter I'll introduce you to the fundamental building blocks of portfolio construction.

A carefully designed portfolio is essential to effective long-term investing. First and foremost, your portfolio strategy should be designed around your emotional tolerance for loss. It should also systematically take into account additional factors, including: your investment time horizon, family budget, net worth, personal health, family goals, inheritance likelihood and occupation.

Practical knowledge of the fundamentals of prudent investing is critical to financial literacy. Without some understanding of how risk can be controlled with portfolio design, an investor's fear of loss may cause her to shy away from participating in the securities markets altogether.

Other investors may have the opposite problem: A tendency to think of investing as a form of gambling, where the game is to guess which stocks will quickly rise in value, ride them while they're hot, and jettison them before they plummet back down. This sort of gambling mentality can lead to frequent transactions, higher costs, and higher taxes, all of which can erode the value of the investor's portfolio. In most cases, frequent trading delivers lackluster long term performance. Myriad studies have shown that it is very difficult to consistently predict when stock prices are going to rise or fall.

Neither an uninformed fear of loss nor an aggressive gambling mentality is likely to lead to investing success. Failure to understand prudent investing principles can drastically compromise your ability to offset the long-term impact of inflation on savings, or to build a nest egg sufficient to fund retirement needs.

Chasing Performance: Not a Recipe for Success

One of the most challenging tasks of a financial planner is convincing clients to diversify into asset classes or mutual funds that may not be doing well at the current moment. Investors have a natural inclination to build a portfolio by searching for stocks or mutual funds that are "hot" now — that have shown strong recent performance.

One of the essential maxims of successful investing, which I'm sure you've heard before, is to buy "low" and sell "high." This sounds easier to do that it actually is! Chasing funds, stocks or asset classes that are currently hot is very tempting, but it can, and frequently does lead investors to buy "high" and sell "low", the opposite of what is desired.

Although occasionally a fast rising stock or superstar mutual fund will continue to do well *after you buy it* (not likely if you are familiar with Murphy's Law), there are many reasons not to simply select investments based on recent, or short-term performance. Later in this chapter I'll discuss the statistical advantages of portfolio diversification.

Sometimes real world examples pack a more powerful punch than reasoned mathematical arguments! For instance, imagine that you bought stock mutual funds based on terrific recent performance just before either of the two huge and sudden stock market drops that occurred during the period from 2001 to 2002, and in 2008. The results could have been devastating.

To help you understand that the hot asset class of today will inevitably be replaced by another one, it may be helpful to describe a type of chart many Financial Planners use, displaying the annual returns of different classes of stocks and bonds, going back several decades.

Ibbotson Associates is a company that publishes this type of information. Their historical asset performance grids are laid out with each year in a separate column. You can find an example of this type of chart by searching the internet for an <u>Ibbotson asset allocation chart</u>.

Each column is comprised of colored boxes, with each box representing a different asset class. The asset class boxes in each column are ranked in order of their relative performance during the year. A quick look at the chart will show a checkerboard pattern—no two consecutive years will show the same hierarchy of asset class performance.

For example, in 2001 the Russell 2000 Value Index, representing small domestic companies with lower ratios of stock prices to earnings per share (P/E ratio), finished in the top category.

Meanwhile, the MSCI EAFE Index, representing Japan and industrialized European countries, finished last. Results in 2007 were nearly the opposite of those from 2001; the Russell 2000 finished dead last and the MSCI EAFE Index ended the year in second place.

Related to the self-defeating tendency of investors to chase performance is the willingness of some to believe that there are experts who can predict and pinpoint which asset class or category is going to be the best each year.

Of course we can't fault the investor exclusively for this gullibility — the investment environment is filled with marketing messages suggesting that certain firms or individuals can help investors pick next month's or next year's biggest winners.

The reality is that determining exactly which sector of the economy is going to do best next year is extremely difficult to do — especially over and over again, year after year. Investors relying on someone with crystal ball-like foresight to tell them which sector or asset class to pick each year are unlikely to attain their financial goals.

It takes time to be a successful investor. For most people, the best approach is to hold a carefully chosen mix of assets in your portfolio, some of which will "zig" when others "zag." We call this creating a diversified portfolio.

Holding a group of funds that don't all react the same way to financial events can even out the fluctuations in your total portfolio and help you make steady, less volatile progress toward your savings goals.

Experience shows that investors with less volatile portfolios are less likely to experience losses sharp enough to trigger capitulation and abandonment of their investment strategy.

The Impact of Human Behavior on Investing Results

In March 2010, *Dalbar Inc.*, a widely respected firm that studies investor behavior, issued the results of its study of investment performance.

The research showed that over the 20-year period ending December 31, 2009, the average stock investor earned an average of 3.17 percent per year, while the average performance of an index of large U.S. stocks averaged 8.2 percent. That's a huge disparity.

In the press release, Lou Harvey, the president of *Dalbar* said:

> "…the original QAIB findings still hold true: Mutual fund investors do not achieve the returns cited by fund firms due to their irrational behavior."

John Bogle the founder of *Vanguard Funds*, calls this tendency of investors to hurt themselves by making poor investment choices the great unspoken secret of investing.

What causes this huge disconnect in real world investor performance? One of the main reasons appears to be excessive trading.

Another cause of poor returns is a tendency for novice or poorly educated investors to fall prey to the herd mentality—they do whatever they believe everyone else is doing.

Holding a group of funds that don't all react the same way to financial events can even out the fluctuations in your total portfolio and help you make steady, less volatile progress toward your savings goals.

Historically, when "everyone" is jumping on a particular bandwagon, it's usually a sign that circumstances are about to change, sometimes drastically, and people late to the party can get hurt the most. Following the investing crowd can result in buying high, just before a market downturn, or selling low, just before a market rally.

A great teachable moment was the cataclysmic residential real estate bust of 2008. Remember how unanimous the chorus of: Buy! Buy! Buy! and Refi! Refi! Refi!! was in 2005, 2006 and 2007? Millions of people who followed the herd in those days lost a significant portion of their net worth due to depreciating real estate values. Even worse, many of these people are stuck with mortgage debt exceeding the current value of their homes.

Behavioral finance is a popular field of academic inquiry. It is crucial that financial professionals learn how to help their clients develop healthy saving and investing behaviors. Simply discussing theoretical strategies is not sufficient. Investors need hands-on experience using basic financial planning tools to help them adopt healthier financial behaviors.

The predilection of investors to both act impulsively and to follow popular investing trends can have a profound negative impact on their investment success. One of the most important services Financial Planners can provide to their clients is the counseling needed to help investors avoid these twin behavioral pitfalls.

Investors need a systematic approach to investing, and most will do best by working with a Financial Planner to put together a diversified portfolio of five to 15 different high quality active or passive funds.

Maintenance of the portfolio requires regular review of the individual funds, periodic rebalancing, and adjustment the portfolio when personal risk tolerance factors change.

In the following pages I'll describe a scientific approach to building personalized investment portfolios. This process begins with the collection of information and an assessment of the investor's risk tolerance. Then, using principles of diversification, correlation, performance and volatility, a portfolio template appropriate to the investor's circumstances, risk tolerance and goals can be constructed.

Construction of the Portfolio Template

Risk Tolerance

You and/or your Financial Planner will take a detailed look at the facts of your financial circumstances, assess your *objective* and *subjective* risk tolerance factors, and then reach agreement about the proper degree of risk in your portfolio.

This process begins by collecting information about your financial circumstances on an Investment Questionnaire (example on page 151, Appendix C).

For the purpose of assessing your objective risk tolerance, the questionnaire captures objective facts, such as your total assets, liquid assets, income, expenses, and the nature and quantity of your invested assets apart from the portfolio being considered. Anticipated future changes to any of these values will also be considered.

Assessing objective risk tolerance also requires that you answer several more speculative questions, such as: How long do you intend to let an account grow before you will need to withdraw the money and begin to use it? How long will you need to take income in retirement, and how much income per year will you need?

To arrive at plausibly accurate answers to these questions, you and your Financial Planner must carefully consider factors such as your current occupation, career aspirations, potential inheritances, family goals, and family and personal health history.

Several other key elements of your financial planning circumstances need to be carefully considered. How long will you be able to invest for growth *before* you begin to take withdrawals from your account for income? How much income will be needed per year after withdrawals begin?

What would be a practical assumption about your (and your spouse's) life expectancy? Life expectancy is important, because it suggests the length of the time during which you will be making withdrawals, which in turn has an impact on the amount of money you need to accumulate *before* income is taken.

Subjective risk tolerance addresses your emotional tolerance for investment losses. Investment questionnaires usually include questions that allow you to provide nuanced answers to questions that address subjective risk tolerance. You may be asked to predict a point at which a loss of portfolio value would be so emotionally painful that you would exit the stock market entirely.

To find what Financial Planners call the investor's "capitulation point," the questionnaire might ask how you think you would respond to account losses of certain magnitudes. For example, imagine that you begin your investment process with an initial amount of $10,000.

Let's assume your theoretical investment account's performance was generally in line with that of financial markets, and dropped to $8,000 (that's a 20 percent loss for people who are math-challenged) in a year's time.

In the face of such a loss, would you succumb to fear and terminate your investment program (capitulate), or would you "ride it out," believing that given enough time, markets should recover the losses and eventually deliver a solid positive rate of return?

An investor with a low subjective risk tolerance might respond to this type of question by declaring that even a 10 percent (or $1,000) loss would be intolerable. Such an investor should have a relatively conservative portfolio comprised primarily of stable, non-volatile assets, and focus on asset combinations that reduce volatility.

A realistic goal for such a strategy would be to generate a better net return than what could be expected from "risk-free" investments such as bank Certificates of Deposit or 90-day US Treasury Bills.

Risk tolerance is anything but a perfect science: Subjective risk tolerance in particular changes quickly and unpredictably, and cannot be measured with absolute accuracy — after all, it's based on emotions!

Who can predict with utter certainty *what* their reaction would be to losing 20 percent of an investment portfolio over a short period of time?

Marriage, childbirth, a job promotion, or a realization that investment portfolio losses cause more anxiety than anticipated, are life events representing potentially significant changes to an investor's risk tolerance.

At regular intervals after the investment process is implemented, an investor should periodically review both objective and subjective risk tolerance factors. If significant changes have occurred in either area, it may be prudent to make adjustments to the investment strategy.

Aggressive investors should understand that it may take quite a while for a portfolio to recover after large losses are incurred. For example, if you were fully invested in large cap domestic stocks in 2008 and lost 37 percent of $100,000, dropping the account value to $63,000, then followed this with a gain of 27 percent in 2009, you would still be far short of recovering 100 percent of the original investment.

Here's another example, underscoring how important it is to think clearly when evaluating investment losses and gains: After losing 50 percent, an investor must earn 100 percent to recover her losses. (50 percent of $100,000 equals $50,000, and 100 percent of $50,000 also equals $50,000). If this doesn't make sense to you, a Financial Planner will be able to illustrate this concept for you in terms you understand.

The stock market turmoil we experienced at both ends of this recent decade underscored for me how damaging large losses can be to investors, particularly older people with shorter time horizons who may have less time to replenish their retirement nest egg with new earnings.

Investors with shorter time horizons should think very carefully about how aggressive their portfolios should be, and what adjustments they will be willing to make if losses accumulate.

> *Marriage, childbirth, a job promotion, or a realization that investment portfolio losses cause more anxiety than anticipated, are life events representing potentially significant changes to an investor's risk tolerance.*

Matching Portfolio Risk to Investor Risk Tolerance

Now that we've discussed the steps that need to be taken to assess investor risk tolerance, the next phase of the process involves matching the design of the investment portfolio to the investor's risk tolerance. This is done with the help of Portfolio Optimization software that combines historical asset performance data and the investor's risk tolerance information to create an optimized portfolio template.

The portfolio template divides the investor's portfolio among various asset classes for diversification purposes. The classic primary asset classes are stocks, bonds and cash. Most investors today will sub-divide the stock and bond portions of the portfolio into subcategories to achieve additional diversification.

Newer software programs may diversify an investor's portfolio even further over additional asset classes such as real estate, commodities, currencies, hedge fund strategies, and private equity.

Portfolio optimization software scores or quantifies an investor's risk tolerance using the answers the investor provides on the Investment Questionnaire.

This score is translated into a volatility statistic, representing how much negative portfolio fluctuation an investor can tolerate without capitulating, or giving up on her investment program. The volatility statistic is used as a boundary when the software generates an optimal mix of assets in the form of a portfolio template.

The optimization software uses something called "back-testing" to create the portfolio template. "Back-testing" refers to calculations made by the software as it searches for the combination of assets that *historically* would have generated the best performance while keeping the portfolio's ups and downs within the limits that correspond to the investor's tolerance for risk/volatility.

Once the software has identified the optimum asset combination for a particular investor, it may also project the average growth rate of the portfolio over the time period that applies to the investor's circumstances (time horizon). Historical asset data is used from a time period in the past that corresponds to your portfolio's future time horizon.

Volatility

Volatility is a very important parameter to consider when designing a portfolio. Certain assets are highly sensitive to daily changes in the economic environment, causing their values to rise and fall more dramatically than other more stable assets.

These more sensitive assets are said to be riskier because their short-term value is harder to predict, and are assigned a higher volatility measurement by the portfolio software.

Examples of asset classes with higher historical volatility (risk characteristics) include small company stocks and stocks of companies based in countries that are still developing, known as "emerging market" countries.

The future prospects of small companies are less certain, and this reality makes their stock prices more volatile than those of large multi-national corporations.

Due to additional economic and political uncertainty, the stock prices of companies based in emerging countries are more volatile than those of companies based in developed countries.

Bonds also have varying risk or volatility characteristics. For example, high yield corporate bonds (bonds issued by smaller, less stable companies) have been historically more volatile than U.S. government bonds.

Time Can Offset Volatility

An aggressive portfolio contains a high percentage of volatile assets, meaning assets that can change quickly in value. However, volatility and strong long-term performance are frequently two sides of the same coin.

It's important to realize that other factors being equal, people with longer time horizons and higher risk tolerances can afford to be more aggressive and include a higher percentage of volatile assets in their portfolios.

This is true because although volatile assets are likely to drop precipitously in value at some point (negative volatility), investors with long time horizons have ample time for assets to eventually recover.

> An aggressive portfolio contains a high percentage of volatile assets, meaning assets that can change quickly in value. However, volatility and strong long-term performance are frequently two sides of the same coin.

Statistically, such an investor should eventually enjoy an offsetting amount of *positive* volatility (rapid growth), ultimately resulting in a higher long-term average rate of return than can be expected from a portfolio of less volatile assets.

This concept can be clearly understood when looking at a 40-year performance chart comparing average prices of small company stocks to those of large company stocks. You'll notice that the small stock graph fluctuates a lot more than the large stock graph, but at the end of the forty years the total increase in value of small stocks is substantially higher than that of large stocks.

People in their 20s and 30s are assumed to have a higher objective risk tolerance than people in their 50s. An investor in his mid-20s has an investment time horizon several decades longer than that of a Baby Boomer.

This extra time is very important. It can help him offset the high volatility of an aggressive portfolio with the extra time needed to even out the gyrations in portfolio value and reap the higher long-range average returns expected from a more volatile (risky) portfolio.

Another maxim of investing is that an investor should eventually be rewarded for taking more risk. Here the key is the word 'eventually'; in some cases it may take quite a while to receive the reward!

When your time horizon for a particular investment is short, it is smart to avoid or minimize exposure to highly volatile investments. The value of volatile investments could drop suddenly, just before you need the money, leaving you with insufficient time for the portfolio to recover.

Risk Disclosures

Investments in stocks, bonds, mutual funds and exchange traded funds are subject to market risk, including the possible loss of principal invested. Investors should carefully consider their investment objectives, their risk tolerance and the individual risk/reward attributes of any fund, individual stock or bond instrument considered for investment.

Additionally, before investing in a fund, investors should read the fund prospectus carefully and make sure they understand the risks and objectives of the fund, as well as the internal fund costs and potential transaction costs when buying or selling shares of the fund. Fund prospectuses are available online from the fund company offering the fund, or by mail if requested.

Always remember that an investor's shares, once redeemed, may be worth more or less than the original cost, and that current fund performance may be lower or higher than shown in historical performance data.

Diversification May Reduce, But Does Not Eliminate Risk

Diversification, while important and useful as a way to manage risk in a portfolio, does not eliminate risk, does not assure a profit, and does not guarantee against loss in a declining market.

Managing Portfolio Risk/Volatility Using Diversification

The concept of Portfolio Diversification can be further divided into Quantitative Diversification and Correlation Diversification.

Quantitative Diversification is based on the principle that there is safety in numbers. Instead of buying one large domestic technology company's stock, you can spread the same amount of money over a *group* of large domestic technology stocks.

This allows you to enjoy an investment result that represents the average performance of the group while avoiding the risk of sharp investment declines due to a dramatic drop in a single company's stock price.

Believe me, there are a multitude of examples of companies that seemingly could do no wrong, only to suddenly fall from grace and suffer rapidly falling stock prices.

Earlier, I explained why mutual fund and ETF investing is a solid starting point for your investment dollars. Investing in these funds is a simple way to achieve quantitative diversification, particularly if you begin with a modest sum.

One fund can contain as many as 100 different stocks, bonds, or both. You can buy shares of some funds with as little as $25.

When you buy shares of a fund, it means that you own a small fragment of every stock or bond contained within that fund. Thus you have already achieved some level of diversification by spreading your money over multiple companies.

An investor can achieve additional diversification by building a portfolio of several funds that cover different areas of the bond and stock market.

You may ask, "Why not focus on one fund that seems to have the best chance of earning consistent high returns?"

A single fund is unlikely to offer sufficient diversification for the long-term investor.

This is because most funds specialize in a particular *kind* of bond or stock, and actively managed funds pick their stocks and bonds using a particular system.

When adverse economic events occur, entire categories of stocks or bonds, or stock picking systems may suffer. So yes, a single fund provides some diversification, but one fund rarely provides sufficient quantitative diversification for an entire portfolio.

Correlation Diversification refers to spreading the money in your portfolio among various types of assets, each of which reacts differently to changes in the investing environment and to the ups and downs of business cycles.

NEGATIVE CORRELATION means that historically, when one asset class moves in one direction, the other asset class moves in the opposite direction.

If two asset classes *move by the same amount* in opposite directions, they are said to be highly negatively correlated. The inclusion of asset classes with high negative correlation to each other can be very useful in reducing total portfolio fluctuation.

LOW CORRELATION means that there does not appear to be a strong positive *or* negative relationship between two asset classes.

A truly diversified portfolio typically contains a mix of assets with low correlation as well as others with high negative correlation to each other.

It should be clear now that it takes more than a few calculations on the back of a cocktail napkin to ascertain what the right mix of assets is likely to be for a particular investor.

Financial Planners use software that captures the degree to which each asset class has had a high, low, positive or negative correlation to other asset classes in the past.

By spreading your portfolio over asset classes that do not respond in the same way to economic stimuli (inflation, international political conflict, shortages of commodities, recession, etc.), you may be able to reduce the portfolio's overall volatility, *without* drastically reducing performance.

Another way to summarize the purpose of diversification is to say: Financial Planners look for the combination of assets likely to deliver the best portfolio performance without gyrating so much that the investor abandons her investment plan.

Diversification Trade-offs

A rational concern when discussing diversification is that it may lead to weaker or "watered down" performance, compared to simply concentrating your portfolio on the asset class that historically has shown the best long term performance. In some cases, this may well be true! However, done well, strategic diversification offers many benefits.

I like to say that strong performance and volatility are two sides of the same coin — you cannot have the first without the second. Volatility means variation in return from one short period to another. A highly volatile asset could be up 40 percent one year and down 35 percent the next.

Volatility can make grown men cry! No matter how high your self-proclaimed risk tolerance, witnessing a huge drop in your account values over a short period of time can be terrifying.

Financial Planners advocate some asset class diversification for all but the most risk tolerant investors.

The first reason for this is that many investors overestimate their emotional or subjective risk tolerance, and may be tempted to abandon their investment strategy after dramatic losses in a year like 2008.

When people capitulate to fear and pull out of the stock market after steep losses, they usually miss most of the recovery, truly wreaking havoc on their long term savings plans.

Another important reason for diversification has to do with the fundamental inability to predict with total assurance how various asset classes are going to perform in the future.

Do you really want to put all of your "eggs" in one "basket" (asset class)? What if future relative asset class performance differs substantially from what we've seen in the past? What if you suddenly need to withdraw money earlier than anticipated?

A detailed discussion of the fine points of volatility and the impacts of diversification and asset correlation on portfolio construction is beyond the scope and purpose of this book.

The point to remember is that effective diversification can smooth out the ups and downs of month to month portfolio performance without severely reducing long term growth rates. This is what we mean by improving the *efficiency* of the portfolio.

Improved portfolio efficiency means increasing the amount of performance per unit of risk/volatility embedded in the portfolio design, based on historical data.

One way to achieve correlation diversification on a simplified level is to hold a classic mix of stocks, bonds and money-market funds.

The rational investor is willing to accept a small performance sacrifice in exchange for a much greater proportional reduction in volatility. Reducing volatility increases portfolio growth-rate certainty, and enhances investor peace of mind — no small feat.

Simplified Diversification

One way to achieve correlation diversification on a simplified level is to hold a classic mix of stocks, bonds and money-market funds. These are three asset classes that in general have negative or no correlation to each other.

Before the advent of portfolio optimization software, investors diversified their investments over these three fundamental asset classes to calibrate the volatility of their portfolios. If you only had five minutes to design your investment portfolio, there are a few basic strategies you could use in order to create a basic, "rule of thumb" risk-adjusted portfolio.

First, in the interest of time, stick with the three classic asset classes:

1 Stocks
2 Bonds
3 Money-Market Funds (Cash)

Ancient texts recommend that a prudent investor spread her investments equally among three classic asset types that match to an interesting degree the different attributes of stocks, bonds and cash/money market funds.

Today's investing environment is vastly more complicated than it was thousands of years ago, but this ancient advice has the ring of common sense to it.

Money-market funds represent an asset class that is very likely to be stable. Stocks represent an asset class that is volatile and speculative, but which over time can generate the most growth.

Bonds represent an asset class that pays income on a regular basis, is less volatile than stock, but has less long-term growth potential than stock.

Money that may be needed soon should be invested in something very stable such as money-market funds or bank deposits. Long-term investors may want to focus primarily on stocks and bonds.

Second, it makes sense to use funds to acquire basic quantitative diversification.

Third, a long term investor may want to use some version of a time-honored investing rule of thumb, which states that the percentage of bonds in your portfolio should roughly equal your age. Another way to express this concept is to say that the percentage of stock in your portfolio should equal the number 100 minus your age.

The reasoning behind this rule is that as you age, your investment time horizon diminishes, and you should gradually reduce volatility in your portfolio. This rule of thumb does not capture individual investor nuance, but it is not a bad place to begin.

Reducing portfolio volatility means reducing the percentage of volatile assets (like small company domestic or emerging market stocks) held in the portfolio, and replacing them with more stable asset classes like short-term government bonds, or highly rated corporate and/or municipal bonds.

Due to extended life expectancies, some Financial Planners now recommend adjusting the rule of thumb to say that an investor's stock percentage should equal 110 minus his age.

Other Planners who favor more frequent portfolio adjustments based on current economic circumstances may not have much use for this rule of thumb.

Also, since women have longer life expectancies than men, some financial professionals recommend that when adjusting for age, women should hold five percent more stock in their portfolios than the percentage that would be recommended for a man in similar financial circumstances.

Diversification: The Portfolio Optimization Frontier

To get a statistical edge, newer Portfolio Optimization software programs increase and refine diversification by adding additional asset classes such as commodities, currencies, real estate related assets and even certain hedge fund strategies.

In some cases, back-testing of these more diversified portfolio strategies show potential for enhanced performance and reduced volatility compared to what can be achieved using only stocks, bonds and cash.

Not only are more asset classes being incorporated into today's Portfolio Optimization software, but new portfolio management strategies are being contemplated.

Financial Planners are looking for ways to take advantage of recent research indicating that correlation between asset classes fluctuates dramatically when market volatility changes.

Those who tout this new research claim that it could:

1 Help new software programs improve the application of historical asset class back-testing when designing current portfolios,
2 Tailor initial portfolios more appropriately to the economic circumstances that exist at portfolio inception, and
3 Develop tactical portfolio strategies and methodologies that would modify the portfolio asset ratios more frequently based on current economic events, as well as real time asset performance, asset volatility and correlation data.

This new research does not represent an enormous departure from traditional portfolio design and management strategies, but it is significant, and worthy of further study. Disadvantages of software-driven dynamic asset allocation (semi-frequent trading strategies) include higher transaction fees and unfavorable tax consequences.

It will take time for the Financial Planning profession and the larger investing community to fully evaluate these new ideas. It remains to be seen if they can deliver substantial improvements in *net* long-term portfolio performance and/or reduced volatility.

Probability-Based Portfolio Management

Portfolio optimization involves *projecting* future asset performance based upon past performance of those assets. Since the future invariably ends up being different from the past, portfolio optimization is by definition a speculative exercise.

You may understandably ask: *If using past performance to guide future investment strategy is speculative, why bother with Portfolio Optimization at all?*

The simple answer is that this process can substantially increase the *probability* that your investment goals will be reached. Using a sophisticated data-driven framework will help you adapt to changes in personal circumstances and financial markets as the future unfolds.

I like to use the concept of probability when discussing various areas of financial planning. This concept helps people understand right away that the projections and statistics Financial Planners use to help clients plan their future and manage their investments are educated guesses — not guarantees.

Portfolio Optimization software may project an average rate of growth for the portfolio over the time horizon being discussed.

Investors should understand immediately that this is an estimate. It is important for you, the investor, to know how sensitive these pro-jections — and your actual results — will be to real world fluctuations in asset values.

Probability analysis and modeling of unusual or extreme future financial scenarios (high inflation, deflation, credit crunches, declining real estate values, etc.) can help us understand the *sensitivity* of our projected portfolio outcomes to changes in market conditions.

Highly volatile/sensitive portfolios are less predictable than more conservative portfolios over a specific time period, because their poten-tial variance from the mean or average rate of return — a volatility measurement called standard deviation — is large.

Investors with very long time horizons (such as people in their 20's and early 30's), have a better chance of enjoying the potential high returns that may be attainable with a volatile (aggressive) portfolio.

The problem for investors with volatile portfolios and shorter time horizons is that one or two years of unusually poor performance could have a big negative impact on the portfolio's average growth rate and the amount of money the investor ultimately ends up with at the end of the investment period.

Investors who need aggressive, volatile portfolios generating high rates of return to attain retirement goals have a lower probability of success than do investors with accumulation goals and investing behaviors that make it possible for them to get to where they want to go using more conservative portfolios.

Once this concept of probability is fully explained and illustrated, the investor may realize that one way to increase her probability of success is by investing more money during the accumulation period.

This change in investing behavior could allow her to use a less aggressive portfolio design, which in turn increases her probability of success in attaining a specific savings goal.

> *Investors who need aggressive, volatile portfolios generating high rates of return to attain retirement goals have a lower probability of success than do investors with accumulation goals and investing behaviors that make it possible for them to get to where they want to go using more conservative portfolios.*

This is where the investment portfolio strategy discussion can lead back into a larger discussion about how the investor's current financial behavior — savings and spending — will ultimately impact the income she has available at retirement.

Simply defining what investing success means to the investor can be a very enlightening experience. She may choose to make some life-style sacrifices now to increase her chances of being able to support her desired life style in retirement.

Would you be satisfied with an 85 percent probability that your investments will earn 6 percent per year over 20 years, or would you rather be more aggressive and reach for an average annual return of 7.5 percent, even though the probability of success drops to 69 percent?

These are not easy questions to answer, and your feelings about risk and probability may change dramatically as your life unfolds.

This is why, as time goes on, it's important to periodically make sure that your portfolio is *still* aligned with your goals and circumstances. You and your Financial Planner should be prepared to adjust your portfolio when significant changes take place in your life.

Thinking and planning in terms of probabilities can help you be a better investor. Once you understand that using historical asset data to predict the *future* behavior of these assets has limitations, you can focus on the fundamental goal of crafting a realistic investment strategy.

Generally speaking, the best portfolio design has a high probability of success and is not likely to push you past your risk tolerance boundaries on the journey towards an enjoyable and fulfilling retirement.

Modeling

Unpredictable events will inevitably occur in your personal life and in the external investing environment. One goal of thorough financial planning is preparation — taking steps to ensure that you, the client/investor have a familiarity with adjustments that can be made when significant personal changes occur in your life.

Sometimes the best "adjustment" will be to your own emotional reaction to events; a reminder to yourself to continue to think long-term and avoid making an impulsive change to your portfolio that could be counterproductive.

For the benefit of their clients (and themselves) Financial Planners will sometimes use Portfolio Optimization software to "model" the theoretical impact of unusual events on client portfolios.

The investor is able to preview, or have a simulated experience of what could happen to his portfolio under various conditions (high inflation, dramatic stock losses, etc.). The reality is that low probability events occur, just with less frequency, and no portfolio of securities is immune from the impact of unexpected events.

Running through unusual "what if" scenarios can help the investor feel more in control of his investing experience. This, in turn, may help him "inoculate" himself against extremes of emotion or impulsive reactions when disruptive events occur.

Summary: Portfolio Optimization Software

There are many different kinds of Portfolio Optimization software, and you might ask your Financial Planner to describe the limiting factors of one version versus another.

Some software programs include more asset classes than others do, and some reach back further into history to mine performance data.

Some of the newest programs analyze historical data in increasingly complex ways, using algorithms to more accurately mirror or capture the behavior of portfolios under unusual or extreme circumstances.

Generally speaking, the best portfolio design has a high probability of success and is not likely to push you past your risk tolerance boundaries on the journey towards an enjoyable and fulfilling retirement.

Even the best software cannot provide you with ironclad guarantees of future results.

This fact underscores the value of working with an experienced Financial Planner. Experience, technical knowledge, timing and even luck inevitably enter the portfolio construction process.

A strong working relationship with the right person can help you understand which elements of the process you can control, as well as how to adapt to circumstances that are beyond your control.

Portfolio Template Adjustments

Generating an investment portfolio template is a very useful initial step in the investment process. A Financial Planner may recommend adjustments to the initial template based on expected future macro-economic trends that do not show up in data from prior decades, or on certain aspects of the client's risk tolerance profile that may not be captured by the investment questionnaire.

Goal Setting

As part of the financial planning process, most individuals or families will establish a target savings goal; a nest egg amount to be attained by a certain date.

Portfolio Optimization software can help the investor integrate his investment risk tolerance and his financial (savings) behavior with his long-range savings objective, by illustrating the trade offs between investment risk/volatility and projected portfolio performance.

The savings accumulation goal can serve as either a hard target, directly influencing investment strategy and against which savings behavior and progress can be periodically measured, or as a "softer" goal, representing lifetime aspirations.

Having a specific savings goal and timeline helps the investor and Financial Planner measure progress and can serve as a strong investor incentive to modify financial behavior when progress toward the goal is falling short of expectations.

In the opposite case — when progress toward a goal is ahead of expectations — probability-based investing can suggest reducing the riskiness of the investment portfolio to increase the likelihood that the savings goal will be attained. Annual reviews can be a perfect time to discuss these issues.

Sometimes an investor is disappointed by the projected growth rate generated initially by the portfolio software.

Maybe the risk tolerance answers he provided caused the software to recommend a more conservative portfolio design than he anticipated.

Should he go back into the software and change his risk tolerance score, modifying the portfolio template to be more aggressive to increase his projected growth rate?

Doing this can be either productive or dangerous, depending on whether the investor can truly withstand the potential negative repercussions of increasing his portfolio's volatility.

As I mentioned earlier in this book, behavioral finance research indicates that investors are prone to overestimating their future tolerance for risk (meaning short-term losses).

It is also important to remember that generally the more aggressive the portfolio design, the lower the probability that the investor's actual future investment outcomes will match the software projections.

An investor has other clear choices when faced with the likelihood that the risk-adjusted portfolio recommended by the software will not result in the desired amount of accumulated savings at a particular time or age.

He could choose to save more money and increase contributions to his portfolio; accept a lower target accumulation amount at a specified age; or aim for the same target goal, but at a later age, giving his portfolio more time to reach the goal.

There's no absolute right or wrong here. From the Financial Planner's perspective, it's a matter of helping each investor explore options and ultimately settle on an approach that is the best fit for his current circumstances and mind set. Moreover, one approach can replace another as time goes on and the investor's circumstances evolve.

On-Going Portfolio Management

Periodic Review of Your Portfolio is Critical

Although holding mutual funds (or stocks) with strong long-term track records can add an important element of stability to your portfolio, all securities in the portfolio should be reviewed at regular intervals.

Actively managed mutual funds, in particular, must be carefully monitored. Fund managers can depart, leaving different people at the helm who were not responsible for the fund's stellar track record. Or, a fund's management team can make an investment decision based on a long-term objective or expectation, causing the fund's short-term performance to lag its past performance.

Internal changes within actively managed mutual funds are not the only source of unintended portfolio disruption. Another type of dynamic change can be referred to as "correlation creep." This occurs when asset classes that historically have been negatively or non-correlated become more positively correlated over time.

Potential causes of correlation creep include advances in trading technology and information sharing, and expansion of stock exchanges to every corner of the world.

Moreover, correlation between asset classes can increase dramatically when securities markets experience high volatility, as we saw in 2008.

Correlation creep can result in reduced diversification and cause unexpected volatility in your portfolio. It's important for the investor to realize that vigilance is required when managing an investment portfolio.

Consider having a Financial Planner periodically use up-to-date software to review the volatility profile of your portfolio and make sure it still matches up well with your personal risk tolerance factors.

Although one of the goals of this book is to avoid diving too deeply into the smaller details of investing, I will touch on several prudent portfolio management practices worth mentioning, as well as strategies that can be used to address potential portfolio challenges.

Rebalancing

An investor might initiate an investment program with a moderate risk portfolio comprised of 50 percent stock, 40 percent bonds and 10 percent money market funds.

Inevitably, there will come a time when one or more of the funds in the portfolio has substantially outpaced the others, or one entire asset class will have outperformed the others.

A dramatic rise or fall in the value of one fund or an asset class can dramatically skew the basic ratio of stocks to bonds, changing the risk characteristics of the portfolio.

On a smaller scale, the value of one type of stock or bond relative to another could also have a significant impact on the combined attributes of the portfolio.

For example, if an investor had begun an investment program in March 2009 allocating 50 percent of the portfolio to stock funds, it is likely that the stock portion would have dramatically outperformed the bond and cash portions by April 2010.

At this point the stock portion could have grown to 60 percent or even 70 percent of the portfolio. The portfolio would have become distorted compared to the original template, and its new configuration may no longer match the investor's risk tolerance.

"Rebalancing" means restoring the asset ratios in your portfolio after distortion has occurred. This is done by selling assets that have increased in relative value, and buying more of the assets that have declined in value.

Consider having a Financial Planner periodically use up-to-date software to review the volatility profile of your portfolio and make sure it still matches up well with your personal risk tolerance factors.

Recent studies indicate that it may be wise not to rebalance more than once or twice a year, since strong asset growth trends tend to continue for months before subsiding.

Statistically this likelihood offsets the dangers of allowing your portfolio asset ratios to depart from the original parameters for short periods of time. This is another example of how historical research can help investors find a balance between competing considerations.

"Black Swan" Events

A "Black Swan Event" is a dramatic metaphor for a highly unusual occurrence, and it's been used recently to describe the near-collapse of the international financial system in 2008.

There have been two enormous stock market collapses in just the last twelve years. Highly unusual? Yes. Impossible? Of course not. Highly unusual events will occur, and no system or individual has shown an infallible ability to predict when they will happen, what the full impact on the investment world will be, or how long the impact will last.

Portfolio Optimization software manipulates historical asset data to create a portfolio that is calibrated to an investor's tolerance for volatility (sudden losses), but may not be able to encompass the risks posed by Black Swan events.

Current software may take statistical shortcuts and "smooth" the data, eliminating highly unusual instances of extreme volatility. Twenty years or less of data is often used.

Twenty years sounds like a long time, and two decades of changes in asset values does generate a lot of data, but in the grand scheme of things it is still a limited period equal to only about 1/4 of a modern life expectancy.

Additionally, we are always challenged by looking at the past to predict the future. Without question there will be significant changes in the investing environment over the next 20 years, changes that may not be easily anticipated when looking at data from the past.

When designing appropriate portfolios, Financial Planners must take into account, and adjust to, the limitations and conventions of the portfolio design software. Financial Planners must remind investors that even the best software can only deal in probabilities, not certainties.

Inevitably the financial planning industry will incorporate more statistical information into Portfolio Optimization software as the data capacity and speed of the software programs improves. Even when it does, however, projections will still be just that: projections, or educated guesses. The goal is to have these guesses be as educated as possible!

Given these limitations, it's very clear that when a highly unusual financial system event *does* occur, the investor's portfolio volatility may exceed his risk tolerance boundaries. This is in fact what happened to many investors during the stock market collapses of 2001-2002 and 2008, in some cases driving distraught investors away from the securities markets all together.

All of this variability, together with recent history and the limitations of the tools we have available, leads me to conclude that sometimes in the investing world all bets are off.

No matter how carefully a portfolio is constructed, there is some possibility that the investor will be threatened with losses exceeding his risk-tolerance.

No matter how carefully a portfolio is constructed, there is some possibility that the investor will be threatened with losses exceeding his risk-tolerance.

Although recent experience has shown that many investors who "stayed the course" and remained in the market after these recent market drops recovered most or all of their losses, there is no iron-clad guarantee that a similar rapid recovery will happen the next time we are faced with a so-called Black Swan event.

Loss-Threshold Agreement

One way to address this hard to quantify "risk" can be called a *loss-threshold agreement.*

You and your Financial Planner could agree ahead of time on a loss threshold that would prompt a decision to liquidate significant portions of the portfolio and "park" the proceeds in a stable or principal guaranteed investment, such as an insured money market account or bank CD.

This concept will be considered investment heresy by traditionalists, many of whom believe that when a portfolio is correctly calibrated, and investor circumstances are stable, the investor should never, *ever* sell because of market losses.

Nevertheless, I think the concept should be considered. This loss-threshold could change over time if your life circumstances undergo a significant change or if your portfolio's progress has been unusually successful (or for that matter, unusually unsuccessful!).

For example, if your portfolio grows faster than expected, or, conversely, lags the expected growth rate, you might adjust your loss-threshold.

Your threshold could increase if you had built up a "cushion" of gains, or diminish if you feel that your cushion has eroded, reducing your risk tolerance.

Financial professionals skeptical about this approach might correctly point out that the disadvantages of this strategy include additional transaction costs and possible adverse tax consequences.

An even bigger challenge would be the need to pick a time to buy back into the markets to re-establish your portfolio. Once you have sold out of stocks or other assets, it becomes difficult to choose a time for reentry that ultimately rewards you for exiting the market in the first place.

While agreeing that there are potential disadvantages to the loss-threshold agreement strategy, my experience helping clients manage money has shown me that rare events of the sort we have recently witnessed can severely damage an investor's confidence and seriously jeopardize his long-range financial plan.

In such cases, it may be most important to "stop the bleeding" and stabilize the portfolio. Otherwise investors incurring losses much greater than anticipated may abandon the securities markets for good.

This would be even more destructive to an investor's financial future than missing part of a market recovery by temporarily shifting money from securities to a stable asset such as a money market fund.

Personal investing has everything to do with human psychology and behavior, not just the dry details of investment gains and losses.

When and if to make changes to portfolios in the teeth of sharp and prolonged market drops are among the most difficult judgment calls a Financial Planner or investor will ever have to make.

It is worth noting that since the 2008 stock market and financial system debacle, more financial planners and professional money managers are questioning the rigidity and practicality of the buy-and-hold (forever) philosophy, and experimenting with other approaches.

Tax Issues: Managing Pre-Tax and After-Tax Portfolios

Within retirement accounts (IRAs, 401(k) Plans, etc.), there are no immediate tax consequences when profits are taken, or dividend and interest payments are generated.

These *pre-tax* accounts are allowed to grow without current taxation, temporarily protected by the retirement plan "wrapper."

It is only when withdrawals are made from a retirement account that income taxes may be due.

Taxes do become an issue in non-retirement accounts (called *after-tax* accounts because the original investment is made with money that has already been taxed).

When mutual funds held inside *after-tax* accounts sell fund assets, or the fund receives dividends or interest payments, account holders incur tax consequences. Also, account holders selling shares of mutual funds within their after-tax accounts will incur taxable gains or losses.

In a **NON-RETIREMENT AFTER-TAX ACCOUNT**, an investor might do well to follow certain tax-sensitive rules for portfolio management:

- Populate your after-tax portfolio with a higher percentage of passively managed index mutual funds. Managers of index funds do not buy and sell fund holdings nearly as frequently as do managers of actively managed funds.
- When you do select actively managed mutual funds, look for those with lower "turnover ratios." Lower turnover

means that the funds tend to hold their stocks and bonds longer before selling, thereby limiting current taxation.

- Opt for less buying and selling of funds in your non-retirement accounts by selecting fewer funds, and by selecting funds that can prudently be held for longer periods of time.
- Near the end of the year, review the portfolio and consider "harvesting" tax losses (selling assets that have lost value) to offset realized gains that could lead to current taxation.

Tax Characteristics of Investment Accounts

Investors should always consider how taxation will affect their investment strategies.

People who are consistently in a high tax bracket should look for ways to minimize or even eliminate income taxes on investment earnings. This can be done by favoring the following investment vehicles and/or government sponsored savings programs:

MUNI BONDS: Interest generated from bonds issued by states and municipalities may be federal and state income tax-free under some circumstances.

ROTH IRAS: Contributions to this type of retirement plan are not deductible like most other retirement plans, but profits generated may be received as tax-free income.

529 COLLEGE SAVINGS PLANS: The 529 Plan permits earnings to be withdrawn income tax-free when used for qualifying higher education expenses.

CASH VALUE LIFE INSURANCE POLICIES: Cash values accumulated within life insurance policies can generate tax-free income: When profits are withdrawn they are treated as policy loans as long as the policy is in force.

It is very hard to be a successful investor without a fundamental working knowledge of how tax issues impact investment outcomes.

REMEMBER: It's not what you *make* in your investment portfolio, it's what you *keep* that matters! After the "dust" clears (taxes and fees are paid), how much do you actually have left?

Managing the Portfolio in Real Time

Some portfolio management decisions are judgment calls. The quality of those calls will vary. Don't lose heart if you think you, your Financial Planner or the manager of one of the funds in your portfolio has made a mistake. Try to learn from everything you experience in your investment life, and realize that portfolio management is not a perfect science with a guaranteed outcome.

Another good precept you might want to keep in mind is that it's best not to fall in love with your portfolio holdings. You will be better off taking a rules-based, data-driven approach, which may require an admission that an earlier fund or security purchase has not turned out well, and should be sold.

Summary:

Creating a Diversified, Risk-Adjusted Portfolio

Before you select specific securities or funds, and before you implement the SRI screening process, you should generate a high quality portfolio template with projected volatility that is calibrated not to exceed your risk tolerance. The following is a summary of the steps that you can take to achieve this:

1 Complete a detailed investment Questionnaire by providing objective facts as well as answers to subjective questions, both of which will help establish your tolerance for investment losses and portfolio volatility.

2 Enter this data into Portfolio Optimization software which will generate a portfolio template, specifying a mix of diverse types of assets that, in combination, align with your risk-tolerance and goals. Take note of the projected average growth rate and projected accumulation amount at retirement.

3 Experiment with the software by changing the risk tolerance data entered into the program. This can help you understand the pros and cons of taking more or less risk with your portfolio, and how managing risk can influence the probability that you will attain the projected accumulation goal.

4 Consider whether your projected accumulation goal will be sufficient to fund your retirement and whether your savings habits should be modified.

5 Integrate the information you've acquired, and create the appropriate portfolio template.

Risk Disclosures

Investments in stocks, bonds, mutual funds and exchange traded funds are subject to market risk, including the possible loss of principal invested. Investors should carefully consider their investment objectives, their risk tolerance and the individual risk/reward attributes of any fund, individual stock or bond instrument considered for investment.

Additionally, before investing in a fund, investors should read the fund prospectus carefully and make sure they understand the risks and objectives of the fund, as well as the internal fund costs and potential transaction costs when buying or selling shares of the fund. Fund prospectuses are available online from the fund company offering the fund, or by mail if requested.

Always remember that an investor's shares, once redeemed, may be worth more or less than the original cost, and that current fund performance may be lower or higher than shown in historical performance data.

Diversification

Diversification, while important and useful as a way to manage risk in a portfolio, does not eliminate risk, does not assure a profit, and does not guarantee against loss in a declining market.

CHAPTER 5

Navigating Today's Investing Environment

Information Age — Information Glut

Investors today are exposed to more financial, trading and economic data than ever before. We are also rapidly approaching a 24-hour trading window — soon it will be simple for investors to find a stock exchange somewhere in the world open for business at any time of the day or night.

If harnessed intelligently, this unfettered access to trading information and the world's stock exchanges can empower you, and offer broader opportunities for investment than ever before.

The "dark side" of this huge onslaught of information is that without an effective strategy for sorting through and organizing it, people can feel overwhelmed and unable to make intelligent investing decisions.

Successful investing, with or without the Socially Responsible Investing (SRI) component, requires more than a rudimentary understanding of investment vehicles and effective portfolio construction.

Investors need to know how the investing environment is organized, how to distinguish between various types of financial professionals offering retail services, and how to recognize and manage their own (sometime self-defeating) investment impulses.

The Financial Media Can Hurt as Well as Help Investors

There's no lack of financial media "noise" out there. Today a prodigious amount of economic and financial data, together with interpretive commentary emanates from the television and the internet, updated almost on a minute-to-minute basis.

For the most part, this data is of dubious value to the investor seeking to build a strong, diversified long-term investment portfolio. Think of Shakespeare's phrase: "Much ado about nothing". Much emphasis is placed on daily, even hourly, fluctuations in asset values, as if only someone hovering over a computer keyboard, ready to strike at an opportune moment, can possibly hope to keep up with the pace of the economy.

In reality, all of this stimulation may lead an investor to focus on the proverbial trees instead of the forest. Too much attention on short-term asset fluctuations can cause investors to lose sight of the proven strategies for long term investing success.

As I pointed out in Chapter 4, *Dalbar Inc.*, a market research company, found that during the 20 years from 1984 to 2004, the average stock fund investor earned returns of only 3.7 percent per year, while the S&P 500 Index of large American corporate stock prices returned 13.2 percent.

Shockingly, this led to *Dalbar's* conclusion that on an inflation-adjusted basis, the average stock fund investor earned $13,835 on a $100,000 investment made in 1985, while the inflation-adjusted return of the S&P 500 Index would have been $591,337 or 43 times greater.

The reason most often cited for the lackluster performance of individual investors is frequent buying and selling, as they attempt to capture the latest investing trend. This sort of investor behavior generally leads to investment returns that fall far short of long-term market averages.

In other words, the average investor may well be better off holding shares of broadly diversified funds for the long term. Making short-term trades based on the torrent of daily data pumped out by the financial media is not a recipe for success.

TV shows, magazines, websites and newsletters are all vying for investors' attention. These purveyors of financial information and advice exist to sell product and garner revenue from advertisers. TV shows are based around "personalities" who dramatize fluctuations in daily economic data.

It's debatable how useful this "infotainment" is to investors who can easily get the impression that investing is like gambling at a casino or race-track, with fortunes made or lost overnight by betting on the short-term gains or losses of individual stocks or market segments. For the average individual investor, this sort of rapid trading behavior will not lead to successful long-term investing results.

The reason most often cited for the lackluster performance of individual investors is frequent buying and selling, as they attempt to capture the latest investing trend.

Lessons from 2008

You don't have to be a Harvard-trained economist to understand how poorly many of the big financial services firms managed their own companies leading up to the financial meltdown of 2008.

Numerous books and movies have been written over the past couple of years depicting and deconstructing the abysmal judgment of these firms' executives and in-house analysts.

The financial regulatory structure had been systematically eviscerated over the prior decades.

Government regulators failed utterly to warn investors or Wall Street managers about the dangers of excessive leverage, mortgage securitization, the huge real estate "bubble," systemic conflicts of interest or the extent to which Wall Street firms were gambling with opaque derivative investments that their corporate managers didn't fully understand.

Several of the most venerated American financial service corporations self-destructed, and chaos in international financial markets ensued. Only unprecedented intervention by central governments around the globe prevented a financial Armageddon the likes of which hadn't been seen in more than half a century.

Retail banks, investment banks, private equity firms, hedge funds, mortgage brokers, university endowment funds and insurance companies — many of the biggest names in the financial service industry got it dead wrong, and would not be here today without the benefit of massive taxpayer funded bailouts.

Investors should be aware that many of the large banks and financial firms that were on the brink of failure in 2008 are still around, bigger than ever, rebranding themselves with expensive marketing campaigns, and once again promising to provide expert investment advice to their clients.

An oft-quoted witticism states that the definition of insanity is doing the same thing over and over again expecting different results.

Investors would be wise to greet the glib marketing slogans and assurances of investment expertise put forth by large financial institutions with a strong dose of healthy skepticism.

> *Investors would be wise to greet the glib marketing slogans and assurances of investment expertise put forth by large financial institutions with a strong dose of healthy skepticism.*

2012 Postscript

Sadly, many economists are of the opinion that not enough has been accomplished in the way of financial system reform during the intervening several years and counting. A handful of the biggest banks have *actually gotten larger!*

Corporate lobbying in political campaigns has been further deregulated, making it even easier for large financial firms to influence government policy and lobby for watered-down financial regulation.

Profound conflicts of interest among and within market participants continue to exist. Ratings agencies, crucial arbiters of risk in financial markets, *continue* to be paid by the very firms they are supposed to evaluate. Certain types of derivative investments, representing *hundreds* of trillions of dollars of risk, are still traded almost completely in private.

Congress has recently implemented a round of financial reforms. However, as has happened before, it's quite possible that the crushing political influence of huge financial institutions will limit or hinder the practical enforcement of the new rules and regulations.

Knowing this, how optimistic can we be that these recent reforms will assure the long term stability of the financial system, limit systemic risk, root out corruption and improve market transparency?

In 2010, we saw market behavior influenced in unpredictable ways by new technology (super-fast programmed trading platforms) and the rapid adoption of new types of trading vehicles (ETFs).

Analysts suspect that regulators are scrambling to understand these and other innovations, and are constantly playing "catch-up" as they adjust the regulatory structure to assure market stability and guard against new opportunities for market manipulation.

What does this have to do with the individual investor?

It's useful for investors to realize that market structure, investment tools, regulation and trading protocols are all constantly evolving, making it even more of a challenge for an individual investor to navigate the investing environment on her own.

This level of market complexity also suggests that many investors would do well to enlist the assistance of an experienced Financial Planner.

Counter-Intuitive Investor Behavior

Despite massive losses suffered in 2008 by many who invested with and in the big financial firms, the data show that relatively few individual investors took what was left of their accounts elsewhere.

Why do you think that is? I was initially stunned by this startling reluctance of investors to seek better financial advice, but eventually, after reflecting on what I've observed about human nature, this phenomenon began to make more sense.

First, let's face it: Humans are herd animals. I know many of us fancy ourselves to be courageous individualists, forever striking out on our own where others fear to tread. This is demonstrably not true in the world of investing.

We humans frequently opt for the "devil we know", instead of trying something brand new, even if our rational minds implore us to do otherwise! Emotions are very powerful, and we are frequently drawn to things that are familiar, especially when knowledge of the reasons for success or failure of a particular course of action is limited.

This apparent counter-intuitive investor behavior seen in 2008 may also have something to do with the complexity of the financial services industry, and with the difficulty investors have in sorting out the pros and cons of different approaches to investing.

People can feel lost when confronted by the prospect of trying to find a new advisor. What criteria should they use? Who can be trusted?

People can feel lost when confronted by the prospect of trying to find a new advisor. What criteria should they use? Who can be trusted?

If investors feel incapable of making clear distinctions between different types of financial services, or the professionals who provide them, they may default to maintaining current relationships, rather than acknowledging their dissatisfaction and reaching out to unfamiliar financial professionals.

Also, as I said earlier, being bombarded with short-term financial data and differing opinions from commentators can actually make it more difficult for investors to sort out their options. Any of these cognitive and emotional challenges cited above can lead to inertia and reluctance to make a change.

Big Brand Marketing Captured Your Attention Years Ago

By "Big Brands" I mean the national banking, insurance and financial firms that spend tens of millions of dollars to deliver advertising on radio, television, and the internet; sponsor high profile sporting events; and promulgate the logos and jingles we know so well.

Representatives and agents employed by Big Brand firms may be more interested in selling the firm's products than scouring the investing landscape for the best possible investment products and least expensive trading strategies for their clients.

Big Brand firm employees may have more allegiance to corporate sales goals than to professional goals of providing the best possible advice and ongoing service to each customer.

In essence, many of these financial professionals are glorified salespeople representing their parent corporations' products. This is not automatically a bad thing as long as it is disclosed to you, the potential client, before you make a decision to work with such an individual. There is nothing wrong with being a salesman as long as you don't try to pretend to be something else — such as a financial professional offering objective advice and guidance.

It's important to remember that you, the client, are first and foremost a profit center for the Big Brand firm, and that corporations naturally seek to maximize revenue *from* each client. Again, there is nothing inherently wrong with this way of offering financial services, as long as it made very clear what the financial professional's objectives are.

Another reality of these huge financial firms is that as a client, it is easy to get lost in the crowd.

These multi-national corporations have millions of clients and offices all over the world. Their multi-million dollar marketing campaigns and skyscrapers branded with neon logos attract a constant flow of new clients.

Big Brand financial firms, like other large corporations, are focused on immediate bottom line revenue. Management can be expected to look for ways to minimize the "cost" of doing business with the public.

Some firms may do this by emphasizing more profitable proprietary products, standardizing products and services offered, and by devising strategies that minimize the time spent by the experienced reps with customers after they have become clients.

In some cases, firms can effectively sell mediocre products or products with high fees and expenses because their relentless national advertising campaigns and potent branding efforts attract clients who leave their healthy skepticism at the door.

Meet Your Big Brand Financial Firm Advisor

People hired by the big financial firms to be on the front lines, selling the firm's brand, products and services directly to the general public *are chosen and promoted precisely for their ability to bond with you, the prospect, and persuade you to become a client.*

Whether or not these people are masters of the technical knowledge needed to help you develop a successful investment program, they are typically expert at convincing you that they and their firm really do have your best interests at heart.

When you encounter one of these "top salespeople," the person will undoubtedly be very friendly, exude self-confidence and be well dressed.

His elegant, well-appointed office might feature plaques acknowledging his selfless community activities. Colorful photographs of his happy prosperous family may adorn the gleaming bookcases and mahogany desk.

More bluntly, the people working for these firms are professional sales people of a high caliber. The wealthier you appear to be, the more likely it is that you will be introduced to one of the firm's most persuasive representatives.

This is what you are up against when you walk through the doors of a Big Brand financial firm: The crème de la crème of salespeople, with an enormous marketing budget behind them and all the resources necessary to make them appear friendly, authoritative, clever and successful.

The next time you find yourself being wooed by someone from one of these organizations, please don't forget the hard-earned lessons of 2008.

Perception is not always reality.

I am not on a mission to automatically discredit anyone who is housed and exclusively employed by one of these multi-national financial firms, but I do want to remind you, the investor, to look carefully behind the glossy corporate image and carefully discern the substance and quality of what is truly being offered.

Financial Professionals: What Do Their Licenses Mean?

More than a few investors have encountered a financial professional who initially seemed trustworthy, only to be revealed later as nothing more than a sales person looking for an opportunity to sell you the highest commission product he could find.

Government and industry regulators struggle to police the interaction between financial professionals and the public, but this is a battle that is never over. Charlatans and scam artists will never disappear completely from the financial services industry, or any other nook or cranny of human endeavor, for that matter.

In some cases it's not the full-time scam artist who hurts you: It could just be someone who needs one more sale to meet his manager's monthly expectations, or an ambitious insurance agent eager to trumpet his next big deal to his girlfriend.

When regulators try to turn up the heat and enforce more stringent disclosure rules, inevitably there will be push-back from powerful industry lobbying groups warning against imposing "too much regulation" that might negatively impact corporate profit margins.

This is the way of the marketplace. In a perfect world, these opposing forces would negotiate compromises, balancing the interests of all parties concerned.

In today's world, clearly far from perfect, industry lobbyists have tremendous political clout, and consequently have a hugely disproportionate impact on the nature of the financial services environment encountered by the public.

I mention this to you so that you are alert to the need to use your own common sense and a heaping portion of healthy skepticism when venturing out into the financial services arena.

Please do not expect regulators to automatically protect you from deceptive sales practices or flawed investment schemes, and don't assume that those documents you are being asked to sign have been carefully vetted by experts with your best interests at heart.

The subject of regulation leads naturally to another substantial problem in our industry: Confusion over the meaning and usefulness of the many licenses, titles and designations held or used by financial professionals.

Licensing, Standards of Care, Compensation and Regulation

The following pages deal with possibly the most mind-numbing aspects of the financial services environment! I will make an effort to provide some clarification around these confusing distinctions.

Licenses require the passing of written tests, authorize professionals to provide certain services to the public, and are an important aspect of the regulatory framework within which the professionals operate.

They are an indicator of the level of knowledge possessed by the financial professional. Licenses also dictate how the financial professional may be compensated for services provided.

Advanced Designations are another category of financial service credentials. The legitimate ones are similar to advanced degrees in academia, and when held by a financial professional, indicate additional breadth and depth of knowledge of particular aspects of financial planning.

Since Advanced Designations are awarded by educational enterprises — not by government regulators — the informed Green investor will do well to research the nature of such Advanced Designations.

Most broker/dealers now only permit their registered representatives to display Advanced Designations that have been approved by them and found to represent the legitimate acquisition of useful knowledge.

Standards of Care specify the obligations that a financial professional has toward his customers/clients. As the level of professional services offered becomes more sophisticated, licensing examinations cover more information and become more challenging. Standards of Care then become more rigorous for the purpose of holding the financial professional to higher levels of responsibility for protecting the interests of the investing public.

Methods of Compensation fall into three categories: Commissions, Asset-Based Fees and Financial Planning Fees. Professionals at the lower end of the licensing spectrum are usually limited to receiving compensation in the form of commissions.

Higher levels of licensure permit the financial professional to be paid through fees (or commissions). The firm that employs a professional may limit his compensation options.

Licensing

The hierarchy of licenses most relevant to individual consumers runs from the entry level life insurance license through Series 6 and

7 securities licenses, and then to the Series 66 License (sometimes referred to as the Registered Investment Advisor or RIA license).

Insurance companies constitute a large and important segment of the financial services industry. Insurance agents with just this license are authorized to sell only life insurance products that do not subject the owner to stock market risk.

This license permits the sale of insurance products that incorporate an investment or cash value component, as long as the investment element does not expose the owner to market risk.

The first rung on the ladder of securities licenses is the Series 6 license. Securities industry professionals holding this license are regulated according to national standards and must be associated with a broker/dealer who monitors their activities and approves the products they are permitted to sell.

From a risk perspective, the significance of a Series 6 is that the licensed financial professional now has acquired the entry level license enabling him to sell investments that expose the investor to the advantages and disadvantages of market risk.

Series 6 licensed people are called "registered representatives" or just "reps" in industry parlance. They are eligible to earn commissions from selling a limited variety of investments that offer clients access to stock and bond markets.

Investments that incorporate market risk offer more growth *potential* than those that don't, but importantly, market-risk investments do *not* protect the investor against loss of principal.

Reps with only a Series 6 license are limited to the sale of pooled securities such as mutual funds, or mutual fund-like accounts offered within life insurance and annuity products. Pooled securities incorporate some degree of quantitative diversification, and therefore are considered to be less risky than individual securities.

The next step in the licensing hierarchy is a Series 7 license. The Series 7 licensing exam is significantly more rigorous than the Series 6 exam. It covers investment principles in substantial depth, as well as trading protocols used when buying or selling *individual* stocks, bonds or ETFs.

The Series 7 exam training also ensures that licensed individuals have a basic understanding of more complex trading tools and techniques such as options, selling short, and the use of margin accounts to "leverage" an investment strategy by borrowing investment capital from a broker/dealer firm.

> The Series 66 Registered Investment Advisor's Representative license is extremely important. It permits the financial professional to move away from a commission-based compensation system.

The Series 66 Registered Investment Advisor's Representative license is extremely important. It permits the financial professional to move away from a commission-based compensation system. With a Series 66, he is now permitted to receive payment in the form of quarterly asset-based fees (based on a set percentage of the investor's portfolio), or hourly or project-based fees for providing Financial Planning advice.

Standards of Care: "Full Disclosure" and "Suitability"

Standards of care specify the obligations and responsibilities of the financial professional. The Standard of Care hierarchy runs from the lowest standard of "full disclosure" to the slightly more demanding standard called "suitability," and finally to the highest standard, the "fiduciary" standard.

The standard known as "FULL DISCLOSURE" is a relatively low standard sometimes applied to life insurance agents when selling non-securities related life insurance or annuity products. "Full disclosure" can be interpreted to mean that as long as the agent hands the client the mandated disclosure information — often in small print using industry jargon or legalese — and gets the required signatures, the disclosure obligation has been satisfied.

In my opinion, "full disclosure" is at best one small step more rigorous that simply leaving the client or customer to her own devices with an admonition of *buyer beware!*

The next standard in the hierarchy is known as "SUITABILITY". It is by no means the highest standard of care, although this standard provides more protection for the consumer than does "full disclosure." Suitability places a burden on the financial professional to determine if the investment he is recommending to a client is *appropriate*, given what the customer discloses about her circumstances.

As part of this responsibility, the financial professional is required to collect and retain a certain amount of information, assess the information against industry criteria and make a reasonable determination as to whether the purchase of a particular product is appropriate for a specific customer.

Suitability Applied to Mutual Fund Sales

Series 6 and 7 licensed representatives offering securities (market-risk investments) to the general public are at minimum held to the suitability standard.

However, the suitability standard does not necessarily dissuade Series 6 or Series 7 licensed individuals from selling low *quality* investments, such as low performing or high expense mutual funds.

The standard is generally considered satisfied if the *type* of investment sold to the investor is appropriate. In some cases this gives people who work for the Big Brand Firms the freedom to sell the firm's proprietary funds (for example), which may be lackluster or worse, when measured against their peers.

One of the gaping loopholes in the suitability standard is the notion that as long as a particular TYPE of mutual fund is suitable for the investor, the financial professional is free to sell his employer's proprietary product — even if it is a grossly inferior example of that type of product.

The Fiduciary Standard of Care

The highest standard of care is called the **"FIDUCIARY STANDARD."** This is the same standard to which attorneys are held. It requires that financial professionals always put investors' needs ahead of their own.

The fiduciary standard also requires that the financial professional promptly disclose all potential conflicts of interest, compensation arrangements and any other material facts that shed light on the attributes of financial products being considered, or the quality of the financial advice provided.

Some firms shy away from having their employees accept this level of responsibility, possibly because it might hamper the sale of the firm's (less than stellar) proprietary products — many firms' bread and butter.

Currently, industry regulators attempt to make a distinction between the standard of care due from someone who simply helps you, the consumer, purchase a particular financial or insurance product, and the standard of care due from someone who provides investment advice or an overview of your complete financial circumstances.

The predominant industry view is that only someone *primarily* offering advice, and/or advising the client about the totality of their financial circumstances should be held to the higher fiduciary standard, with other transactional relationships defaulting to the less stringent suitability standard. Unfortunately, in the real world this can be a very fuzzy distinction.

If advice was offered, was it *incidental* to the financial transaction? Some industry participants feel that "incidental" advice should not require the assumption of the fiduciary standard of care. Industry trade groups and regulators continue to discuss, refine and negotiate the application of different standards of care to different types of financial transactions.

Registered Investment Advisors (RIAs) are organizations offering investment advice, and the financial professionals who market their services are called IARs (Investment Advisor Representatives). IARs must have a Series 66 license, and are required to accept the fiduciary standard of care when offering their services to the public.

Methods of Compensation

When a financial professional holds nothing but an insurance license, the only mode of payment he may receive is a commission. The insurance industry is very different from the securities industry, and the vast majority of insurance products are sold on a *commission* basis.

Some individuals holding a Life license also hold a Series 6 or 7. This licensing combination allows the agent/representative to sell *variable products* — annuities and life insurance policies — that offer market-risk investments within the insurance product. These hybrid insurance and securities products are primarily sold on a commission basis.

Financial professionals selling securities while holding only a Series 6 or Series 7 license also face limited compensation options. It is not until a person acquires a Series 66 license and affiliates himself with a Registered Investment Advisor that he is able to get away from the commission or transaction-based compensation paradigm.

I feel it is rarely in the investor's best interest to pay a one time "load" or commission when buying shares of mutual funds. Why pay someone a one-time up-front commission to buy mutual funds for you before the impact of the transaction on your portfolio is clear?

In my opinion, it makes sense to pay a rep in smaller amounts over time for assisting you with investment strategy. Let him earn your loyalty by consistently providing good service, and by proving he knows something about what he is doing!

Most investors seeking advice and investment assistance would do well to seek out professionals employed by Registered Investment Advisory (RIA) firms. These Investment Advisor Representatives hold the Series 66 license, which permits investors to avoid commissions when working with them.

The investor can pay such an individual over time, based on the size of the investment portfolio, and not on the basis of transactions that are made within the portfolio. This is called the *asset-based fee* compensation model.

> In my opinion, it makes sense to pay a rep in smaller amounts over time for assisting you with investment strategy. Let him earn your loyalty by consistently providing good service, and by proving he knows something about what he is doing!

Advisors/Financial Planners who operate this way are said to be *"fee-based"*. A portion of the fee is payable every three months, based on the average size of the portfolio.

Generally these fees range from 1.5 percent to 1 percent per year. This type of compensation arrangement creates a pragmatic incentive that encourages the rep to provide you with excellent service and effective advice.

The investor's objective — account growth — is aligned with the Financial Planner's objective — steady and ultimately increasing fee revenue.

The advisor's fee revenue is calculated as a percentage of the investor's account, and increases or diminishes based on the performance of the investments held in the account.

There is another compensation model available when working with Planners employed by an RIA: The investor can pay an hourly or project-based fee to a Financial Planner who is not directly involved in the purchase or sale of investment assets for the portfolio.

The goal in this relationship is to eliminate potential conflicts of interest.

Under this *"fee-only"* compensation scenario, the mechanics of setting up a trading account and implementing the investment decisions are primarily the responsibility of the client.

Advanced Designations

In addition to the licenses authorizing sales of insurance products, financial products, and financial advice, financial professionals can acquire Advanced Designations. CFP®, CLU, CFA, etc., are indicated by a series of initials after the professional's name.

Advanced Designations can indicate additional training, minimum amounts of experience, ethical commitments, and in some cases higher standards of care.

It is wise for consumers to verify what a particular registered rep's designation actually represents, as well as the integrity of the testing and certification process the professional must satisfy to acquire the designation.

It can sometimes be a challenge for investors to sort out the legitimate advanced designations from those of debatable worth that can simply be purchased after completing an open-book test.

It is always a good idea for an investor to research the meaning of the credentials presented by a financial professional, as well as his compliance history and the general reputation of any organization he represents.

The current CFP® practitioner must master a wide variety of financial planning knowledge, and prove his mastery by passing a difficult two-day proctored exam.

When in doubt, parse the data on the business card, get on the computer and do some investigating on your own.

It is beyond the scope of this book to describe the many different advanced designations an investor might encounter, but I do want to say a few things about the Certified Financial Planner™ designation.

The current CFP® practitioner must master a wide variety of financial planning knowledge, and prove his mastery by passing a difficult two-day proctored exam.

Additionally, a practicing CFP® agrees to be held to the fiduciary standard with regard to the vast majority of his interactions with clients.

Finally, the aspiring CFP® must also satisfy minimum experience and formal education requirements, accept supervision by the Certified Financial Planner Board of Standards (www.cfp.net), pass a background check and comply with additional continuing education requirements.

Authoritative financial publications and industry commentators have declared the CFP® designation to be the ultimate personal financial planning credential.

Having personally experienced the rigor of the qualifying exam, I can attest to the breadth of the knowledge required to earn a passing grade. The pass rate for first time test takers is approximately 61 percent.

One side-note about the CFP® mark: Before 1993, people could procure the CFP® designation without taking the proctored two-day exam.

I think it's fair to say that based strictly on credentials, financial professionals with a pre-1993 CFP® designation do not have the same credibility as do those who have passed the exam since 1993.

A financial professional is, of course, much more than the sum of his credentials, but credentials matter, and this is an important distinction to make.

How Financial Professionals are Regulated

It is well beyond the scope of this book to describe in great detail the ins and outs of the securities markets regulatory structure, but in this section I'll present some basic information to help the reader understand how different participants are regulated.

If the financial professional sells insurance products, he will need to be licensed in each state in which he does business, and then appointed by each insurance company he wishes to represent. He must use only approved sales materials when doing business with clients.

CONSUMER TIP: One quick way to ascertain whether an insurance agent is truly "independent" is to look him up on your state's Insurance Commissioner's website (by license number or name).

You will be able to find a public list of the companies with which he is currently appointed. If he has only been appointed with one or two companies in the past few years, he may not be as independent as he would like you to believe.

Financial professionals offering clients access to securities markets are primarily regulated under a national regulatory structure, and they must be supervised to ensure compliance with these regulations.

Supervision includes monitoring email and regular mail correspondence with clients. Additionally, reps may only use marketing materials that have been pre-approved by the supervising entity.

Services and products offered by a registered representative must be pre-approved by his regulatory organization. Some securities products cannot be sold unless the representative holds a Series 7 securities license. Reps who charge a fee for Financial Advice must hold a Series 66 license and be affiliated with a Registered Investment Advisor.

Registered representatives are provided with a menu of approved products and services by their regulating broker/dealer and/or Registered Investment Advisor.

The supervisory organization provides approved client documents and reviews signed documents for suitability before accounts are opened.

Broker/dealers serve as a buffer between the registered rep and regulatory organizations such as the Securities and Exchange Commission.

The broker/dealer's compliance department ensures that the reps comply with federal regulations. Broker/dealers are in turn supervised by the industry's self-regulatory body, the Financial Industry Regulatory Authority (FINRA).

Some broker/dealers are essentially passive, and do not do much trading or investing of their own. Others are much more aggressive and can possibly run into trouble.

Consumers can inspect the public compliance records of both reps and broker/dealers by going to FINRA's website (www.finra.org).

Some registered representatives are only supervised by a broker/dealer. Others are regulated only by a Registered Investment Advisor, and some reps are affiliated with and regulated by both.

RIAs are regulated based on the dollar amount of the RIA's aggregated client "assets under management". States are the primary regulators for RIAs managing $100 million of assets or less, and the federal Securities and Exchange Commission directly regulates larger RIAs.

Both groups are subject to federal securities laws. These dollar thresholds may change from time to time.

Working Definition of an Independent Advisor (IA)

When I use the phrase *"Independent Advisor,"* I'm describing a financial/insurance professional who can and *does* offer insurance and financial products from a wide range of insurance companies, fund families and other product manufacturers.

In general, financial professionals who meet my definition of Independent Advisor are those whose daily activities are *not* tightly managed under a national or regional sales hierarchy.

Most IAs are *not* housed or provided with a salary by a large financial services corporation.

This type of independence is significant, because financial professionals who are utterly dependent on one large organization are under more pressure to sell proprietary products, and less likely to use their own independent judgment when working with clients.

It's not easy to be crystal clear about this distinction. My advice to you is to consider the information provided in this book, seek out Financial Planners who exhibit independence in the way they conduct their businesses and be a sleuth — *ask a lot of questions!*

Be careful — financial professionals know very well that independence is seen positively by most consumers, and will sometimes "camouflage" their obligations to Big Brand financial firms or large regional sales organizations.

Given high-quality alternatives, why would an investor want to work with someone who represents a limited number of insurance and financial products, or who may be susceptible to organizational pressure to sell you the firm's proprietary products?

Independent Advisors vs. the Big Brand Firms

In many ways, the financial professional I call an 'Independent Advisor' is regulated in fundamentally the same way as those housed by and working exclusively for a Big Brand financial firm. There is a profound difference, however, in how business is actually conducted:

The IA has substantially more freedom to make his own determinations about which products and services to offer, how to market his services and how to interact with his clients.

Moreover, few large firms permit all of their representatives to accept a fiduciary standard of care with their clients — these firms may be afraid that this could hinder the sale of (possibly inferior) proprietary products and services. This is likely to be particularly true of certain insurance companies with "captive" agents, meaning their reps can *only* offer proprietary products.

> Given high-quality alternatives, why would an investor want to work with someone who represents a limited number of insurance and financial products?

There are also several large national financial organizations that allow their employees to brand their offices with a personal name but carefully limit the investment products offered to clients. When you get past the appearance of independence, products and services offered by these firms are dictated by corporate managers.

Many financial professionals start out building their businesses functioning as registered reps working for a large firm.

These firms can provide financial support in the early years (as long as reps meet exacting internal requirements for proprietary product sales and revenue generation).

If these reps survive the rigorous regime of the brand name firm, and after several years are able to successfully build a substantial client base, they may eventually separate from the big firm, taking their clients with them and becoming somewhat independent.

I say 'somewhat' because many times I have seen advisors who got their start with a Big Brand firm, move to a large regional organization that fundamentally still has a big firm corporate mentality.

The advisor may like the move because he has more freedom, or because he receives a higher percentage payout from the parent corporation, but the client experience may not change much.

The Client Experience

The key *disadvantage* for IAs is a marketing disadvantage: They do not have a corporately funded marketing engine constantly bringing them new clients.

Nor do they possess a nationally known logo on their business cards to help establish credibility with the general public. Despite these challenges, Independent Advisors cherish their professional autonomy.

This significant marketing disadvantage for the IA can translate to an advantage for their clients — a more intimate and adhesive bond with the financial professional.

Although each organization is different, the stories I've been told by clients — and by employees of such firms — support the idea that there is such a thing as a typical Big Brand corporate mentality in the financial services industry.

This mentality is exemplified by the absolute focus of large firms' management on short-term bottom-line profits, with the result that customer service costs are always under scrutiny.

To offset prodigious overhead, Big Brand financial firm representatives are goaded to increase production (find more clients and more assets!), and to minimize the time/cost incurred servicing existing clients.

To lower service costs, experienced representatives may be advised to limit client contact after "the deal is closed" (the initial client relationship is established), and to delegate the residual "service work" to underlings.

Clients of these huge organizations may be seen as easily replaceable, and individual relationships with clients may not be the firm's highest priority.

Thus, before an investor allows herself to be impressed by the status of someone who has risen to an exalted position within one of these brand name financial service corporations, it would be wise to determine whether such person is personally capable of addressing the full range of the investor's financial planning concerns.

If the Big Brand rep's success within the firm has been due primarily to salesmanship, he may not be the best person from whom to receive the objective, professional advice desired.

The Independent Advisor client experience is likely to be more personal and intimate than what you'd expect when working with large corporate firms. There is a higher likelihood that the person with whom you began the advisory relationship will continue to be fully accessible to you, and you won't be shunted off to a less experienced support person.

IAs tell me that their client relationship paradigm justifies *additional* time spent with each client! This is not a shocking claim — it's based on the reality of the business. IAs acquire new clients primarily through personal referrals from existing clients. Therefore, many IAs find that they receive more referrals if they spend additional time and energy nurturing relationships with clients.

Big Brand firms may operate from a different perspective — most of their new clients are brought in by multi-million dollar marketing campaigns and relentless corporate branding efforts. Clients may be considered "fungible" — meaning easily replaced.

Access to Information and Financial Planning Tools

Unlike behemoths in other industries (Walmart, etc.) offering tangible consumer products, the Big Brands in the financial services industry do *not* generally offer individual investors lower net costs or better access to investments or investment advice than can be received from IAs.

Why is this true?

First of all, financial service consumers are buying intangibles — professional advice, access to markets and information. They are not buying widgets that become cheaper when they are mass produced overseas.

We are living in the midst of the information revolution. Market data and trading platforms are becoming more accessible every day. Access to information has become democratized — the financial professionals employed by Big Firms have no particular advantage in this area.

Second, a rational investor will seek out non-biased information and financial advice. This fact works *against* big financial service corporations, which may manufacture their own investments and hire their own analysts, setting the stage for potential conflicts of interest.

Third, a multitude of independent organizations offer financial information to the public, in many cases at little or no cost, and untainted by conflicts of interest.

Websites such as *Morningstar.com*, or the finance portals of *Google* or *Yahoo*! offer a great deal of current information to the public.

This largely eliminates any monopoly on advice, or access to markets that in the past may have been enjoyed by the Big Brand firms.

Finally, huge financial firms have such prodigious overhead costs that they need to streamline their product lines, manufacture their own products, favor certain business partners and squeeze as much revenue as possible from their reps, while minimizing client service expenses.

It's no surprise that many Big Brand financial firms expect their representatives to emphasize or "push" investment products created by the firm, or products offered by a short list of other organizations with which the firm has "special" expense reimbursement relationships.

The Big Brand financial firms with huge overhead costs may charge more, while providing less in the way of independent advice than the high quality Independent Advisors in your neighborhood.

These corporations have to maintain profit margins sufficient to pay for their national advertising campaigns and bricks and mortar infrastructure. They frequently house their sales forces and support staff at great cost, within financial district edifices that stretch hundreds of feet up into the sky.

Don't forget about the astounding CEO pay packages that also fit into the corporate overhead equation! Big Brand firm hierarchies must draw enormous amounts of money from sales and operations to cover these outsized expenses.

Independent Advisors can avoid being trapped by this relentless revenue imperative by housing themselves independently, and forgoing the juicy compensation packages these firms offer to their top sales people.

Broker/dealers and Registered Investment Advisors that service Independent Advisors recruit them by offering access to market data, trading systems, and an array of third-party portfolio management systems.

When IAs are aggregated together, this creates economies of scale allowing them to access portfolio optimization software and client management technology competitive with that used in-house by the Big Brand firms.

The IA may also have access to a more diverse group of insurance products and mutual fund families. Big Brand firms frequently limit their reps' options in these areas to concentrate on products with the highest profit margins.

The reverse-paradigm situation in financial services is very important for the consumer to understand. When the product being provided consists of information, access and advice, a huge firm's prices may be higher than those of smaller competitors offering similar products.

The Big Brand financial firms with huge overhead costs may charge more, while providing less in the way of independent advice, than the high quality Independent Advisors in your neighborhood.

The access provided by the Independent Advisor to both a diverse array of high quality investment vehicles and sound investment advice, is comparable to — and potentially less expensive than — that offered by the Big Brand Firm representative.

Investor Recourse in Case of a Dispute

Whether your financial professional is independent or captive to a single organization, you as the client will be required to sign an account document that includes a mandatory arbitration clause.

> *The access provided by the Independent Advisor to both a diverse array of high quality investment vehicles and sound investment advice, is comparable to — and potentially less expensive than — that offered by the Big Brand Firm representative.*

If you have a dispute with a financial professional, whether he is independent or works for a large firm, your main and frequently only recourse is to present your complaint to an arbitration panel.

Lawsuits by investors against firms are generally not effective unless they are part of a class action suit alleging a widespread pattern of bad behavior.

Thus the investor does not automatically have better protection against the misbehavior of a Big Brand firm's financial advisor than he does against that of an Independent Advisor.

Independent Advisors have to affiliate with, and agree to be regulated and supervised by a Broker/Dealer, or a Registered Investment Advisor and its regulator. There are many BDs and RIAs that cater to Independent Advisors.

BDs and RIAs have compliance departments that monitor the Independent Advisor's client communications and whose personnel visit the independent representative's office to audit client records and ensure that record-keeping procedures meet regulatory standards.

Errors and Omissions

One of the ultimate backstops when an investor has a valid complaint against a financial professional is the professional's Errors and Omissions (E&O) insurance policy.

Regardless of whether the professional with whom you work is employed by a big firm or seems to fit the definition of the Independent Advisor, the best way to confirm how much protection his personal E&O policy provides is to verify a current copy of the policy statement.

All legitimate broker/dealers require their affiliated reps to have minimum amounts of E&O coverage.

It is entirely possible that an Independent Advisor has an equal or even higher level of E&O insurance than does someone employed by a Big Brand firm.

Clearinghouses Serve as Custodians for Investor Assets

Custody of assets is yet another area where an investor working with a Big Brand firm's representative does not automatically enjoy a meaningful safety advantage, compared to the investor working with an Independent Advisor. Clearinghouses are a very important but little known part of the securities industry. The clearinghouse is the entity that ultimately has custody of the investor's assets.

Most clearinghouses have their own websites and can provide you with detailed records of account activity that can and should be used to validate the information provided by your representative or his firm.

When the system works properly, this layer of separation is an important enhancement to the safety of the investor's assets.

Bernie Madoff, who bilked thousands of investors out of billions of dollars using a Ponzi scheme, apparently fell into a regulatory category that allowed him to serve as his own clearinghouse and retain custody of his clients' assets.

Investors were not able to easily cross-check the account information he provided on his firm's statements with information from another independent source.

These regulatory loopholes were major contributing factors to Madoff's success in perpetuating his fraudulent enterprise for a surprisingly long period of time. Industry critics do not feel that all of the loopholes exploited by Madoff have yet been eliminated.

Although size is not an automatic guarantee of safety, it is important for investors to understand that clearinghouses that aggregate client assets for many Independent Advisors can be larger than those used by Big Brand financial firms.

Follow Your Money!

The vast majority of investor transactions go smoothly, and the mechanical aspects of the securities industry are strenuously regulated. It is important, however, to realize that when an investor submits a check to be invested in the securities markets, it may pass through as many as four different sets of "hands" before it reaches the market.

I advise investors to be cautious when working with a firm that has as its normal practice the depositing of investor cash into the firm's own account.

A registered representative may deliver the check to his Financial Planning firm's operations department. The funds may then flow through a broker/dealer or parent Registered Investment Advisory firm before ending up in the custody of a clearinghouse.

This can happen in two ways: Either the check is transferred intact by these several entities until it reaches the clearinghouse, or the check is actually deposited with one of the intervening entities, with the expectation that funds will eventually be transferred electronically to the clearinghouse.

I advise investors to be cautious when working with a firm that has as its normal practice the depositing of investor cash into the firm's own account.

When investor checks are made out to the financial planning firm or the broker/dealer (instead of the clearinghouse), numerous problems can arise.

There have been cases of broker/dealers suddenly going bankrupt while temporarily in possession of client funds. On other occasions, unscrupulous individuals working for a broker/dealer have devised ways of siphoning off investor money before it gets to the clearinghouse.

When working with an Independent Advisor who has client checks written directly to a third party clearinghouse, an investor can ensure that her money gets to the clearinghouse by accessing the clearinghouse website and verifying the activity.

Generally, when filling out the initial paperwork to open an account through an Independent Advisor, the application and disclosure documents will refer to a separate clearinghouse that is independent from the advisor and his firm. In most cases, your checks will be made out to the clearinghouse, not the advisor's firm. This adds another layer of separation and safety to the process.

After submitting checks or asset transfer documents, the investor can independently verify account activity by setting up an online password protected account directly with the clearinghouse and cross-checking the clearinghouse information with that provided by the Independent Advisor.

This sort of separation of function and transparency may not be as easy to achieve when working with Big Brand firms, or with large regional firms permitted by regulators to hold client assets in their own accounts (however briefly) before transferring them to the clearinghouse.

Common Sense Due Diligence
for the "Green" Investor:

- Read the financial professional's business card carefully, and ask what organization the person represents, and in what capacity

- Ask about licenses and professional designations shown on the financial professional's card or stationary

- Ask the financial professional whether he will be providing advice or simply selling a product

- Ask the financial professional to help you access "Broker Check" on the industry self-regulatory body's website *(www.FINRA.org)* to see if he or his firm has compliance violations on record

- If you are interested in an insurance product, take the time to visit your state insurance commissioner's website. Use the license number on the agent's business card to access his compliance record, as well as the list of insurance companies he is authorized to represent. Does he represent a variety of different insurance companies or just a couple?

- Ask how the financial professional gets paid (commission, asset based fee, planning fee, combination), and what the payments, fees or commissions are

- If you intend to make securities transactions through a financial professional, clarify whether your check will deposited into the firm's account, or is to be made and conveyed to the clearinghouse

- Ask for information about the clearinghouse used

- Check to see if the Broker/Dealer, Registered Investment Advisor and clearinghouse are members of the Securities Investor Protection Corporation (SIPC), *and* whether these entities have additional insurance protecting investor assets

- Take the time to review the "fine print" on the documents, and don't hesitate to ask the financial professional to explain anything that is unclear

- Ask what sort of after-purchase service you can expect, and specifically with whom you will be working after the initial engagement

We shall require a substantially new manner
of thinking if mankind is to survive.

ALBERT EINSTEIN

CHAPTER 6

Wrapping It Up

The centerpiece of "Green Investing" is the investment screening and selection component — commonly called Socially Responsible Investing (SRI). Knowledge of the investment component alone, however, is not enough. Green investors need additional information to help them successfully navigate today's complex investing environment. Using the information provided in this book, investors can truly go Green, and do all of the following:

- Align their investments with their personal values and core beliefs
- Earn a competitive return
- Learn to build a risk-tested, diversified investment portfolio
- Sort through the manifold complexities and distractions of today's investing environment and find prudent, economical solutions to your investment needs
- Leverage the resources of the professional SRI investing community as fund managers identify corporations with strong growth prospects and socially responsible corporate behavior.

141

- Advocate for additional positive change at some of the world's largest corporations by aggregating your assets with other like-minded individuals under a mutual fund "umbrella."

It is crucial that investors know something about the science of risk-adjusted portfolio design; the different types of investment vehicles available; the costs and fees involved; the different ways investors can open accounts and make trades; and the professional qualifications of those who hold themselves out as investment professionals.

In most cases, investors will improve their chances of success by working with an independent Financial Planner who is experienced in the realm of SRI.

Green Investors should also be aware of certain obstacles to successful investing.

One of these obstacles is the financial media's relentless cascade of information about short-term market movements.

Too much exposure to these television shows and financial magazines can easily lead to the perception that investing is similar to gambling, with clever investors buying and selling to exploit short term price movements.

Another obstacle is the sheer volume of marketing propaganda spawned by Big Brand financial firms.

Ubiquitous corporate branding and relentless ad campaigns persuade investors to "trust" huge institutions to help them manage their money.

It's a mistake to simply accept the services offered by these huge corporations without carefully scrutinizing the investment programs being offered, the quality of the advice available, the fees you will incur, and the availability of SRI options. Details potentially disadvantageous to the SRI investor may be hard to ferret out.

In most cases, investors will improve their chances of success by working with an independent Financial Planner who is experienced in the realm of SRI.

Questions to ponder when considering enlisting the help of a financial professional: Is she truly committed to providing you with advice, or is she essentially a glorified salesperson? What are her professional qualifications? Is she putting your interests ahead of her own?

Investing: One of the Last Bastions of Denial?

People are embracing movements such as recycling, shrinking the carbon footprint and utilizing sustainable energy technology. *What about personal investing?*

There are few aspects of our lives that we cling to more intensely and privately than our investments!

There are few aspects of our lives that we cling to more intensely and privately than our investments!

After all, our nest egg represents fundamental security for ourselves and our loved ones, our hopes and dreams for the future, and the quality of our eventual retirement.

Moreover, our investment accounts are the tangible result of and reward for the years we have spent and the sacrifices we have made working and earning a living.

No wonder it's difficult to consider introducing another potentially controversial element to our investment strategy.

It makes us nervous to use criteria other than pure personal profit potential when investing our hard earned money. Greed is good, right?

Our cultural milieu resonates with the message — overt as well as subliminal — that when it comes to investing, one should be a fierce individualist, a ferocious competitor, totally coldblooded, evaluating any investment opportunity solely on the basis of what it can do for us *today!*

But maybe there is another approach, one that takes into consideration the impact our investing behavior has on the world in which we live.

We now know that investing with social responsibility in mind does not involve financial sacrifice.

My question to you then is this: Why not consider Socially Responsible Investing?

Green Investing is Viable and Rewarding

Green investing, with SRI at its core, involves paying attention to, and even attempting to influence, the behavior of corporations offering stock and bonds to the investing public. I have shared my strategies with you for doing this; it doesn't have to involve an enormous amount of time and work on your behalf.

Many of us are willing to change our behaviors, both large and small, once we are convinced that these changes will be beneficial for ourselves and others.

Whether it is reusing grocery bags, upgrading to more energy efficient home lighting or driving a hybrid automobile, people are searching for new and better ways of doing things that can improve their lives, the lives of their neighbors and the future lives of their children.

Once you understand that using SRI criteria as part of your investment process is not an automatic disadvantage, the wider aspects of the SRI approach become meaningful.

People have different ideas about what constitutes socially-responsible corporate behavior.

The point is that what matters is your definition of "socially responsible" — you can customize your SRI strategy to fit your world view.

Some investors are interested in supporting and profiting from the rapid growth of emerging companies that are focused on "green" technologies in fields such as energy conservation, alternative energy, and recycling.

Others may be more interested in using their investment dollars to encourage large established corporations to embrace "greening" of corporate infrastructure, increase the diversity of gender and racial leadership, and ensure that outsourced manufacturing practices are ethical.

Still other investors think of SRI as chiefly the practice of avoiding companies that offer unhealthful or arguably socially destructive products or services such as alcohol, tobacco, gambling and firearms.

Various religious organizations sponsor fund families that screen investments using criteria that agree with their ethical beliefs.

The point is that what matters is *your* definition of "socially responsible" — you can customize your SRI strategy to fit your world view.

And remember, you don't have to make the transition to SRI all at once!

Take your time — you might start by applying the process I've outlined for you to just a portion of your portfolio.

See how it goes.

My hope is that after reading this book, you will be able to say:

"We hold these truths to be self-evident…"

1 It *is* possible to do well while doing good! We *can* direct our investments to companies that better reflect our values, while earning returns that are competitive with those generated using traditional investing strategies.
2 We do not have to spend inordinate amounts of time to implement an SRI strategy.

As I stated earlier, as of January, 2012, the Calvert Socially Responsibility Index (CALVIN) had a five year track record that is superior to that of the S&P 500 Stock Index (INX).

Media articles published in *Business Week* and elsewhere make it clear that investing based on SRI principles can generate returns competitive with traditional investment practices.

Morningstar, the independent mutual fund ratings company, has called SRI a "free good," meaning that SRI investors do not automatically incur a performance "cost" for utilizing SRI screening strategies.

Approaching Socially Responsible Investing in a comprehensive way — what I call Green Investing — gives investors the tools needed to:

1 Successfully navigate today's complex investing environment
2 Implement an investment program that generates competitive returns
3 Help make the world a better place by supporting the better corporate citizens

Seek a Financial Planner Experienced in Green Investing

SRI fund families are not yet household names. The vast majority of investors have only heard of a few of the huge legacy mutual fund families, none of which emphasize Socially Responsible Investing. This is a common theme in the investing world — a small number of huge firms dominate a particular niche of the industry by virtue of their ability to spend enormous sums on advertising and branding.

There are in fact many lesser known fund families managing hundreds of SRI funds, and many of these funds have excellent track records.

It is helpful to work with a Planner who knows how to identify the best SRI funds, and can show you how to combine a number of them into a strong, diversified, risk adjusted portfolio.

In today's challenging and constantly evolving investment environment, the expertise, portfolio design tools and systematic approach an experienced Financial Planner can provide may well be worth the fee paid to her.

Next

The following is an action plan that you can begin implementing right now. *What are you waiting for?*

Green Investing Action Plan

1 Using the information and criteria discussed earlier, identify and interview experienced Financial Planners who have Socially Responsible Investing expertise.

2 Ask your Planner candidates specifically if their system or trading "platform" permits them to work with multiple SRI fund families.

3 Discuss each Financial Planner's experience, fee structure, and the standard of care that will apply to your financial relationship.

4 Don't forget the importance of communication: Ask each Planner a few open-ended questions and notice if their communication skills agree with your process for understanding complex subjects.

5 Choose a Planner and decide whether your SRI focus is going to be general or specific. A general focus offers more investment flexibility, but you may have specific goals, such as: avoiding or emphasizing certain industries/countries, advocating for positive change under the umbrella of an activist fund family, or upholding certain ethical or religious principles.

6 Work with your Planner to develop a risk-adjusted portfolio template, tailored to your unique circumstances. The template should specify the percentage of your portfolio to be allocated to each asset class.

7 Discuss the SRI screening process you will use to select funds that fit the asset class categories stipulated by your portfolio template.

8 Review performance and rating information on the SRI funds that appear to be candidates for your portfolio. Decide which funds

are best, and whether you will invest initially in a lump sum or gradually over time.

9   Implement your investment strategy: Minimize transaction expenses and purchase the funds that best meet your SRI criteria.

10 Make arrangements to review your portfolio at regular intervals and possibly rebalance or adjust your strategy if needed.

11 If you notice significant changes occurring in your life circumstances or your own financial and retirement goals, consider reviewing your portfolio strategy with your Financial Planner.

CONCLUDING NOTE TO THE READER

Throughout these pages, I've outlined sound principles of Green Investing, with a robust Sustainable, Socially Responsible Investing process at the core of the Green Investing concept. I've tried to provide a realistic description of today's investing environment, as well as the information and guidance you will need to select a high quality financial services professional who can help you implement your SRI investing strategy.

I hope this book helps you gain enough self-assurance to incorporate your ethical and moral beliefs within your personal investment strategies, adding meaning to this important part of your life while you build financial security for your family and make progress toward your life goals.

REMEMBER

TRUST BUT VERIFY: As much as you may personally like a financial professional, it is very important to verify his/her professional knowledge and compliance record, as well as the nature and quality of the organization he (or she) represents. Can this person offer non-biased access to a wide variety of top quality investment options, as well as effective portfolio design tools and a rigorous SRI screening strategy?

Don't forget: One of the best attributes an investor can have is a healthy dose of skepticism. If you don't understand an investment vehicle or strategy, you should probably avoid it. Famous clichés persist for a reason: If something sounds too good to be true, it probably is!

Human consciousness arose but a minute before midnight on the geological clock. Yet we mayflies try to bend an ancient world to our purposes, ignorant perhaps of the messages buried in its long history. Let us hope that we are still in the early morning of our April day.

STEPHEN JAY GOULD, "OUR ALLOTED LIFETIMES,"
THE PANDA'S THUMB, 1980

Articles and Resources: Low-Carbon, Sustainable, ESG Investing

"*Sustainable Investing Research Suggests No Performance Penalty*" (11-10-2016); "*Does Sustainable Investing Hurt or Help Returns?*" (12-07-2017); and "*5 Big Things About Sustainable Investing in 2017*" (December 21, 2017) were written by John Hale, PhD., CFA, and published by Morningstar, the independent fund rating organization.

"*Funds That Can Put Your Investments on a Low-Carbon Diet*" (10-13-2017) was published in the New York Times.

Prospectuses for the specific funds mentioned in the NYT article can be found at the following web sites: iShares.com; Dimensional.com; EthoETF.com; Parnassus.com; GreenCentury.com.

Potential investors should carefully consider investment objectives, risks, charges and expenses of the investment company when contemplating an investment in any particular fund. This information can be found in the prospectus or the summary prospectus for the funds in which you are interested. Make sure to read the prospectus carefully before investing.

"Sustainable Reality: Understanding the Performance of Sustainable Investing Strategies" (March, 2015) was published by the Morgan Stanley Institute for Sustainable Investing. We enclose the key findings and summary pages, go here for the full report: https://www.morganstanley.com/sustainableinvesting/pdf/sustainable-reality.pdf

5 Big Things About Sustainable Investing in 2017

Jon Hale, Ph.D., CFA ∨

21 Dec 2017

The Trump Effect

After years of increasing momentum for sustainable investing, 2017 began with concerns that the new administration would have a chilling effect on the field's growth.

The concerns had to do with President Donald Trump promising to "bring back coal," roll back Barack Obama's Clean Power Plan, and pull the United States out of the Paris Climate Agreement, all of which, it was feared, could hurt investments in renewable energy and, more broadly, in companies better aligned with the transition to a low-carbon economy.

Another concern was that corporate America would fall into line with Trump's vision to "Make America Great Again" by dropping all pretense that it cared about sustainability issues. Given these concerns, the thinking went, investors might abandon sustainability and move on to other themes.

But that didn't happen. If there was a "Trump effect" at all, it was as a galvanizing force for sustainable investing. Sustainability may resemble an investment theme, but it's broader than that. It's an approach to decision-making, which in the investment context means a long-term focus that's inclusive of stakeholders, that recognizes that the transition to a low-carbon economy will produce winners and losers, and that investors can have an impact on creating a low-carbon global economy that works for more people.

The number of investors adopting that approach continued to grow in 2017. According to a recent Callan report, more foundations in the U.S., especially large ones, and public pension funds began incorporating ESG into their investment processes this year. A Brown Brothers Harriman/ETF.com survey of "sophisticated ETF investors in the U.S." found a dramatic increase in interest in environmental, social, and governance exchange-traded funds this year (51%) versus last year (37%). Retail funds posted a record year of flows, with more than $5.0 billion in net flows through November, compared with an estimated $4.8 billion for all of last year. Twenty-seven new funds and

ETFs were launched. And surveys continue to report high levels of interest in sustainable investing among women and millennials, but also among baby boomers.

As for companies, I saw little evidence of firms abandoning sustainability in 2017. Why would they? A well-managed company understands the need to assess material ESG risks and opportunities facing its business and to incorporate them into its long-term strategy. That understanding is underscored by a redefinition of corporate responsibility, driven by younger employees and women, who are gradually moving into decision-making roles. Which brings me to the second thing about sustainable investing in 2017:

The Fearless Girl

State Street Global Advisors (SSGA) had the marketing coup of the year with its Fearless Girl statue, commissioned on the first anniversary of the launch of the SPDR SSGA Gender Diversity Index ETF (SHE) and placed opposite the Wall Street bull in time for International Women's Day in early March. The statue was such a hit that it has been permitted to remain in place until March 2018--and I suspect it will be there longer than that.

The Fearless Girl served notice that investors are not going to drop the pursuit of gender equality. Just 5% of S&P 500 companies are headed by a female CEO, 20% of board seats are held by women, and 25% of executive and senior level managers are women. (The investment industry doesn't do any better. A Morningstar report this year found that roughly 20% of funds globally have at least one female manager.)

Shareholders focused considerable attention on this issue in their engagements with corporate management this year, submitting 35 diversity resolutions. Only eight came to a vote, while the remainder were withdrawn, an indication that those companies were willing to address the issue in a way that was suitable to concerned shareholders. For the first time, BlackRock (BLK), SSGA, and Vanguard voted in favor of some of these resolutions. Speaking of which, that brings me to the next thing:

The Big Three Ramp Up Their Engagement Activity

As their passive assets under management have grown and they have become the largest shareholders of most large companies, the Big Three of passive investing--BlackRock, SSGA, and Vanguard--have become more rather than less engaged in stewardship activities, according to a Morningstar report released earlier this month.

That may be surprising to some. Passive investors are, in effect, universal owners. They own every company in a market and will own those companies in perpetuity, so, it is said, they should have little incentive to bother with the costs associated with engagement. Despite being the largest shareholders of most companies, passive investors have little leverage with a company to change its behavior because they cannot divest.

So why are the largest passive asset managers getting *more* involved in stewardship activities?

For one thing, they still have a fiduciary duty to their shareholders. Even without the possibility of exiting a position, being among a company's largest shareholders gives the passive asset manager a voice in the way a company is run, advocating for company policies and behavior that can enhance shareholder value. For a large, passive asset manager to ignore that influence would be to shirk its fiduciary duty to its own investors.

Secondly, large passive asset managers have a public responsibility to be active owners. A large passive asset manager that decides to be a passive owner is saying it doesn't care how a company is run and therefore shares in the responsibility for bad corporate behavior. When major instances of corporate mismanagement occur, better to be on record as a shareholder that engaged with the company on the issue than to be a passive owner that by virtue of sitting on the sidelines has further empowered management and weakened the position of other shareholders. This connection is starting to be made more often in media coverage and can result in a reputational hit to asset managers that are passive owners and, conversely, a reputational plus for those that are active owners.

Third, large passive asset managers have a responsibility to exercise systemic stewardship. With their perspective as the largest shareholders of most large companies and as permanent shareholders, they can focus on long-term issues that can help preserve and improve the financial system itself, which would, in turn, enhance long-term shareholder value. That's why they focus on ESG issues like gender diversity in corporate leadership and climate-risk disclosure, which are really about long-term corporate and systemic sustainability. The large passive asset managers can help bring long-term considerations that have traditionally sat just beyond the purview of shareholders and corporate strategists into the present discussion between management and shareholders.

Climate-Risk Disclosure
This is number four on the list, but perhaps the most consequential of all. Led by the aforementioned Big Three, efforts to get companies to disclose the risks they face from climate change gathered force in 2017. It started off with almost unheard-of majority shareholder votes on climate-risk

disclosure resolutions at Exxon Mobil (XOM) and Occidental Petroleum (OXY). It continued with investors' growing support for companies to disclose based on the recommendations of the Task Force on Climate-Related Financial Disclosures, and just last week, on the second anniversary of the signing of the Paris Agreement, a group of global investors launched an initiative called Climate Action 100+ to drive action on climate change among 100 companies that are the world's largest greenhouse gas emitters. Also last week, Exxon announced in an SEC filing that it would follow the recommendation of its shareholders and release information on "energy demand sensitivities, implications of two degree Celsius scenarios, and positioning for a lower-carbon future."

Assuming investors are successful in spurring more companies to take action on climate disclosure, as they've now been with Exxon, their efforts could have a major impact not only for all investors but for companies themselves by enhancing understanding of climate risks. And by spurring companies to better understand their climate risks, these efforts can lead to more firms taking action to reduce their carbon footprints, thereby achieving the broader impact of reducing greenhouse gas emissions in line with the Paris Agreement.

Impact

That brings me to "impact," the fifth big thing of the year for sustainable investing. Impact is a key outcome of sustainable investing, but more attention has been paid in recent years to incorporating ESG analytics in the investment process as a way to enhance financial returns. Impact became a bigger focus this year.

That's a good thing, because if you are interested in sustainable investing, chances are you would like your investments to have environmental and societal impacts alongside competitive financial returns. Indeed, the very idea of sustainable investing is the win-win proposition that it can deliver on both fronts. And that's what resonates with most sustainable investors. In a recent global investor survey of more than 22,000 investors, for example, Schroders found that sustainable investors see positive impact and financial returns going "hand in hand." Two thirds of Americans in the survey said they are interested in sustainable investing mainly for its impact or for both its impact and its financial return. Only one third said they were interested in it for financial return only.

It's important to note that the widespread and still-growing use of ESG analytics in investment decision-making is itself impactful. It signals that sustainability issues are important and encourages companies to take them seriously. When companies take sustainability issues seriously, they believe it will help their business and, in so doing, they will have a broader environmental or societal impact. Those who are invested in public equity strategies that incorporate ESG are having an impact even if their asset managers are using ESG strictly to improve financial performance.

More broadly, the UN Sustainable Development Goals have been widely discussed--and adopted--this year as a framework for assessing impact. Asset managers are doing this by targeting certain goals or by simply identifying which of the 17 goals are supported by investments in their portfolios, and then developing metrics to assess the impact they're having. More asset managers are rightfully emphasizing their stewardship activities as one of the key ways they are delivering impact, and they are figuring out how to improve their reporting on impact to their investors.

Sustainable investing heads into 2018 with continued momentum, focused on delivering impact alongside financial returns.

Jon Hale, Ph.D., CFA does not own shares in any of the securities mentioned above. Find out about Morningstar's editorial policies.

5/25/2018   Welcome to Morningstar Asia – Malaysia

Sustainable Investing Research Suggests No Performance Penalty

Review of academic studies show sustainable/responsible funds perform on par with conventional funds.

Jon Hale | 07/12/16

We know there is a lot of interest in sustainable investing today, particularly among emerging investor groups like women and millennials, who, by some estimates, will soon control upwards of $30 trillion in assets as they amass wealth through earnings and inheritance.

For high levels of interest in sustainable investing to translate into actual investments, financial intermediaries need to step in to help their clients incorporate sustainability into their portfolios. For advisors, planners, and retirement plan fiduciaries, one of the biggest obstacles to sustainable investing is the lingering perception that it has a negative effect on investment performance.

I just completed a review of academic research on the topic and found that the research strongly suggests that there is no performance penalty associated with sustainable investing.

Dozens of studies have been published over the past 15 years addressing the performance question, with researchers studying different time periods, regions, and asset classes and measuring performance in gross, net, and risk-adjusted terms. To be sure, the findings are varied, but when the evidence is accumulated, the vast majority of studies report neutral or mixed outcomes. There are much smaller numbers of clear-cut positive or negative results, although positive outcomes are more frequent than negative outcomes.

The following two charts provide compelling evidence that's consistent with the research findings. The first shows the performance of the oldest sustainable/responsible index, the MSCI KLD 400 Index, formerly called the Domini 400 Social Index) compared with the S&P 500.

5/25/2018   Welcome to Morningstar Asia – Malaysia

Exhibit 1: MSCI KLD 400 Index versus S&P 500

- *source: Morningstar Direct.*

From its 1990 inception through September 2016, the MSCI KLD 400 has actually outperformed the S&P 500 by 81 basis points annualized. Although much of that outperformance occurred during the 1990s, the KLD index has outperformed by 27 basis points annualized over the trailing 10 years, through September.

The second chart shows the cumulative Morningstar Analyst Rating of all funds tagged in our global database as having a "socially conscious" mandate between 2002 and 2016. I included the year-end star rating of every share class as of the end of each calendar year (and used September data for 2016). To avoid biasing the data in favor of surviving--and likely more successful--funds, the data include funds that have since been liquidated or merged away.

Exhibit 2

**Cumulative Morningstar Ratings, 2002-2016
Socially Conscious Funds vs. Fund Universe**

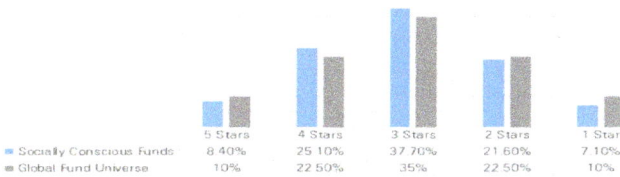

	5 Stars	4 Stars	3 Stars	2 Stars	1 Star
Socially Conscious Funds	8.40%	25.10%	37.70%	21.60%	7.10%
Global Fund Universe	10%	22.50%	35%	22.50%	10%

- *source: Morningstar Direct.*

During that time span, we observe a distribution of Morningstar ratings among socially conscious mutual funds that is similar to that of the overall fund universe. The socially conscious funds cluster slightly more toward the middle (2, 3, and 4 stars) than does the overall universe. It is worth noting, also, the slight positive skew to the star rating distribution of socially conscious funds: more 5-star (8.4%) than 1-star funds (7.1%) and more 4-star (25.1%) than 2-star (21.6%) funds. Thus, the star-ratings results are consistent with the research literature: Socially conscious funds have similar risk-adjusted performance that, if anything, skews positive relative to conventional funds.

While the research is clear that there is not a performance penalty associated with sustainable investing generally, there is some evidence that SRI exclusions, taken in isolation, can be a drag on performance. Few sustainable funds, however, limit themselves to the use of such screens. ssMost funds also use ESG inclusion--the evaluation of company sustainability based on environmental, social, and governance factors either through positive screening or integration of ESG considerations into the stock-selection process. And a growing body of research suggests that ESG inclusion can lead to positive performance outcomes. Thus, with most existing sustainable/responsible funds, the potentially negative effects from SRI exclusions can be offset by the potentially positive effects from using ESG inclusion to select stocks. This line of reasoning suggests that funds that eschew exclusionary screening altogether and rely instead solely on ESG factors may have the most potential to outperform.

For those interested in sustainable investing, the research suggests you can address your sustainability concerns in your portfolios while also receiving competitive performance. To be sure, there remain challenges to sustainable investing. The number of intentionally sustainable funds remains small compared with the overall universe (1% to 2% of funds globally), making it difficult to find funds to fill out a portfolio. (The Morningstar Sustainability Rating for funds can help you find additional funds that hold more-sustainable companies.) And even though such funds perform on par, if not a little better, than conventional funds, there is a range of manager skill and fund quality that investors must still discern when selecting funds, just as they have to do when they are working with the much-larger conventional universe. But there is no reason, based on the academic research on performance, to steer investors away from making sustainability a part of their portfolio.

SUSTAINABILITY MATTERS
Does Sustainable Investing Help or Hurt Returns?

Jon Hale, Ph.D., CFA ⌄

07 Dec 2017

The rationale for sustainable investing makes sense for more and more investors:

- Emphasize material environmental, social, and governance issues that contribute to more-thorough financial analysis
- Focus on the long term, taking into account the impact of decisions on an extended sphere of stakeholders, including the planet itself
- Direct investment to areas that need it as the world transitions to a low-carbon economy
- Encourage more responsible corporate behavior, which makes firms more attractive to talented workers and thus more competitive, enhances intangible value in a social media environment that magnifies corporate missteps, and strengthens confidence in the financial system overall.

But despite that strong rationale, which has attracted trillions in assets under management globally to sustainable investments, one of the main concerns many interested investors still have about sustainable investing is "Will it hurt my returns?"

There are a couple of reasons why this question remains on their minds. First, many consultants and advisors have the misimpression that sustainable investing today is little different than socially responsible investing from two decades ago, which was largely based on aligning portfolios with an investor's values and relied on exclusionary screening based on products or certain kinds of corporate behavior the investor deemed objectionable.

There wasn't a great investment rationale for this approach and it was especially difficult for mutual funds to put together a list of exclusions that would satisfy a large enough number of investors to make the funds viable. This approach was more successful for institutional or individual separate accounts.

Over time, as optimization techniques improved, it become easier for portfolio managers to reduce tracking error caused by exclusions and keep performance competitive. But the negative association remained: If you are excluding companies from your portfolio for non-investment-based reasons, you risk underperforming.

Second, sustainable investing today is not an asset class or even a discrete investment style; there are many ways to do it. Unlike other investment areas that have emerged over the past decade--say, commodities or REITs or frontier markets--you can't readily assess the risk-adjusted returns of "sustainable investing." Alternatives are somewhat analogous insofar as they include different underlying strategies that are similarly hard to evaluate.

Sustainable investing is more of an overarching investment philosophy that supports a wide variety of investment approaches. Sometimes ESG criteria are used to define an investment universe. One manager may exclude the bottom quartile of companies based on ESG evaluations. Another manager may focus on the top third. Others may hone in on the ESG indicators most material to a particular company. In many cases, ESG is integrated alongside other more-traditional financial factors an analyst must consider. Still another approach may focus on companies that are improving their ESG profiles; some may invest in a company with poor ESG credentials if it is priced right. Some funds are "intentional" about sustainability; it's clearly stated in their prospectus. Other funds may be incorporating ESG factors into their investment process without making reference to it in their prospectus. Some strategies still use exclusions, such as those that exclude fossil-fuel companies. Others focus on single themes like low-carbon or gender diversity. There are renewable energy funds and bond funds that focus on social and environmental impact. These approaches could be employed within a passive market-cap-weighted strategy or any number of active strategies, which further complicates performance evaluations.

Finally there are institutional asset owners and asset managers, including giants like BlackRock, State Street Global Advisors, and Vanguard, who are active or have become more active as shareholders on sustainability issues without necessarily incorporating them into their security selection and portfolio construction. This year's proxy season saw asset managers pushing companies to assess and disclose their climate risk to shareholders and to place more women on their boards. They believe companies can enhance shareholder value over the long run by doing these things, but shareholder engagement is not going to be reflected in shorter-term portfolio performance.

With such a variety of approaches to sustainable investing, including those focused on long-term impact that won't show up in returns today, the performance question is impossible to answer with the same level of assurance that you can with strategies based on asset classes or conventional investment styles.

One of the most straightforward ways to assess performance is to compare the performance of public mutual funds and exchange-traded funds that have sustainable intent based on their prospectuses with that of the broader universe. As you can see in Exhibit 1, funds that use ESG criteria or pursue sustainability themes perform well compared with their Morningstar Category peers on a risk-adjusted basis. The current distribution of Morningstar Ratings among sustainable investing funds is skewed in a positive direction, suggesting better risk-adjusted performance. Just above 42% of sustainable funds have 4 or 5 stars, while only 21% have 1 or 2 stars. Based on the normal distribution of the star rating, those numbers should be equal at approximately 33%. The positive skew holds for U.S. Morningstar Style Box categories, non-U.S. stock categories, and bond categories.

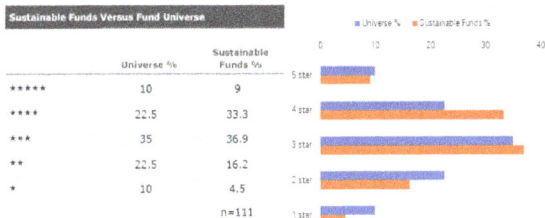

Sustainable Funds Versus Fund Universe

	Universe %	Sustainable Funds %
★★★★★	10	9
★★★★	22.5	33.3
★★★	35	36.9
★★	22.5	16.2
★	10	4.5
		n = 111

Source: Morningstar Direct Data through November 2017

This result is all the more impressive given the variety of different approaches to sustainable investing and, of course, the fact that individual fund managers have different skill sets. It suggests that strategies that focus intentionally on some aspect of sustainable investing, on the whole, don't just hold their own, they outperform the overall universe. Over the long haul, given the compelling rationale for sustainable investing, I expect its performance profile to improve, but you never know-- adoption of sustainable investing principles, in whole or in part, could become so ubiquitous that teasing out performance could remain a challenge. If you want to adopt sustainable investing as your investment philosophy, chances are you can find strategies that will meet your performance expectations.

The New York Times

Funds That Can Put Your Investments on a Low-Carbon Diet

By Tim Gray

Oct. 13, 2017

If you care about climate change, your money can help shrink your carbon footprint. You can buy appliances that are more energy efficient or a hybrid or electric car — or, better yet, a bike. You can install thicker insulation in your home or solar panels on your roof.

But investing in mutual and exchange-traded funds in ways that prioritize climate worries has been harder. Plenty of funds make environmental impact a factor in stock assessments, but few have proclaimed loudly that greenhouse gas emissions are a primary concern, and that has been a problem for investors committed to divesting from fossil fuels.

The smog has begun to clear. A spate of stock funds and E.T.F.s has appeared over the past several years that shun major fossil-fuel producers, like oil drillers and coal miners, or those with excessive greenhouse gas emissions. Carbon dioxide, spewed out mainly by the burning of fossil fuel, accounts for most of such emissions, so these new offerings often call themselves "low carbon."

Now there is a tool, the website Fossil Free Funds, that helps pinpoint funds and E.T.F.s focused on companies withsmaller carbon footprints. "There were 10 funds when we started that we identified as fossil-fuel free," said Andrew S. Behar, chief executive officer of As You Sow, the Oakland, Calif., environmental group that created Fossil Free Funds. "Now it's up to 31."

Fossil Free Funds sprang from Mr. Behar's effort to determine the carbon footprints of the funds in As You Sow's own retirement plan. The exercise showed him how tough it was to piece together the needed information. So he and a colleague, Andrew Montes, created the website, which began in 2015.

The site combines Morningstar data on stock holdings with screens like the Carbon Underground 200, a global index of coal, natural gas and oil companies. If a user types, say, "Vanguard's S.&P. 500 index fund" into the site's search box, a report is generated. That report shows that 21 companies, including Exxon Mobil and Chevron, and 4.28 percent of the fund's total assets overlap with the Carbon Underground 200. That means, of $10,000 invested in the fund, $428 will end up in fossil-fuel stocks.

In contrast, the site's report on the SPDR S.&P. 500 Fossil Fuel Reserves Free E.T.F. shows no overlap. As the E.T.F.'s name suggests, that lack of fossil fuel overlap is intentional.

"What this fund is doing is giving investors the S.&P. 500 minus companies that own reserves of crude oil, natural gas and thermal coal that are economically and technically recoverable," said Christopher C. McKnett, who leads environmental, social and governance strategy for State Street Global Advisors, the E.T.F.'s sponsor. The fund does not exclude reserves of metallurgical coal, which is used in the making of steel, but it does exclude utilities if they own their own reserves, he said. State Street created the E.T.F. for investors committed to divesting from fossil-fuel stocks, Mr. McKnett said.

Another State Street offering, the SPDR MSCI ACWI Low Carbon Target E.T.F., takes a different approach. Rather than barring companies, it favors energy and utility companies with smaller fossil-fuel reserves and lower carbon emissions. The fund is designed to replicate the world market as closely as possible — it invests globally, in developed and developing countries — while still being low carbon, Mr. McKnett said.

Blackrock's iShares MSCI ACWI Low Carbon Target E.T.F. is constructed similarly. Sarah Lee Kjellberg, head of iShares Sustainable E.T.F.s, said Blackrock created the fund partly at the request of institutional investors and financial advisers seeking a low-carbon offering that could serve as someone's core investment. "They're telling us, 'We're trying to strike a balance between providing market exposure and addressing the risk of climate change in our portfolios,'" she said.

A newer low-carbon E.T.F., the Etho Climate Leadership E.T.F., ranks companies according to their carbon efficiency, based on emissions per dollar invested. "We start by analyzing 6,000 companies globally of all capitalization sizes and distill them down to leaders in each industry," said Ian E. Monroe, president and chief sustainability officer of Etho Capital, the fund's sponsor. Mr. Monroe said the goal was not just to ditch big carbon-belchers and fossil-fuel behemoths but also to identify better-run companies. The fund, which began in late 2015, beat the S.&P. 500 last year and so far has done so this year.

Several long-established sponsors of socially screened funds can also help put your portfolio on low-carb diet.

Dimensional Fund Advisors offers two funds that make emissions and fossil-fuel reserves central considerations: the US Sustainability Core 1 Portfolio and International Sustainability Core 1 Portfolio. "Sustainability means different things to different people," said Joseph H. Chi, the company's co-head of portfolio management. "But what we've found is a focus on carbon is one thing people agree on."

When assembling the portfolios, Dimensional applies its usual financial metrics to companies, but it also assesses their emissions, Mr. Chi said. "Our approach is to rank companies both on an absolute basis and against their peers," he said. The portfolio managers then eliminate the those with the worst emissions, de-emphasize the lesser performers and overweight the better ones. Dimensional's one absolute climate-related exclusion is coal companies.

The list of climate sinners is longer at Parnassus Investments and Green Century Capital Management, two specialists in so-called socially responsible funds.

Both the Parnassus Fund and Parnassus Endeavor avoid companies involved in exploration, extraction, production, manufacturing or refining of fossil fuels. That effectively means the portfolio managers avoid the energy and utility sectors, said Ian E. Sexsmith, co-manager of the Parnassus Fund. They do this because some clients haveasked for fossil-free offerings and because of the managers' skepticism about the longer-term prospects of these industries, Mr. Sexsmith said. "As our world becomes more energy efficient and we get better at using alternatives," he said, "we think the energy sector is going to underperform."

Green Century likewise tries to eliminate fossil-fuel companies from its Green Century Equity Fund and Green Century International Index Fund, said Leslie Samuelrich, Green Century's president. The funds, passively managed indexed offerings, impose hard exclusions on coal, gas and oil, companies and on any utility that burns coal.

A group of environmental nonprofits started Green Century in 1991 and it has long avoided the fossil-fuel industry, but its marketing did not highlight that until recently.

"We didn't use the words 'fossil fuel free' till five years ago," Ms. Samuelrich said. "But the demand started to pick up, and we realized we should tell people. So we started promoting that, and since then, our assets have more than doubled," lately reaching $491 million for the company's three funds. Green Century also has a balanced fund that contains bonds as well as stocks.

The variety of low-carbon stock funds makes it easier for people to invest this way. Whether they should invest this way, from a financial standpoint, remains a subject of debate. Investment orthodoxy says that limiting your pool of investments stunts your potential return.

Jon F. Hale, director of sustainability research at Morningstar, said he doubted that people with well-diversified portfolios would see much of an impact on performance if they replaced, say, a conventional domestic, large-capitalization fund with a low-carbon one. A diverse portfolio, he said, would include funds spanning domestic and international markets, large- and small-capitalization stocks and developed and developing countries.

Mr. Hale said the returns of the low-carbon fund would not track the broader market: If the energy sector were to surge, the fund would probably underperform. But, he added, "There's a possibility of a positive return, too." That could happen if the world's economy continues to move toward greater energy efficiency and a greater reliance on renewable sources like wind and solar power.

Personal values have a place in investment decisions, Mr. Hale said, adding that some people viewed divestment from coal, gas and oil as a matter of morals, not money.

"I may be fine with the possibility of my portfolio performing a little less without fossil fuels because I want to add my voice to this movement or feel good about myself," he said. "I may be willing trade off some of the other investment benefits for that."

A version of this article appears in print on October 15, 2017, on Page BU11 of the New York edition with the headline: A Low-Carbon Diet for Investments

Morgan Stanley
Institute for Sustainable Investing

Sustainable Reality:

Understanding the Performance of Sustainable Investment Strategies

A growing number of investors are exploring sustainable investing. In 2012, $1 out of every $9 of US assets under professional management was invested in some form of sustainable investment, primarily in public equities. In 2014 that number increased to $1 out of every $6 – to a total of $6.57 trillion now invested sustainably.[1]

With this growth, investors increasingly ask what tradeoffs, if any, there are to sustainable investing. Some investors believe sustainable investments underperform, or have higher risk than their traditional counterparts.

We set out to explore whether this view is accurate.

Key Findings

- Investing in sustainability has usually met, and often exceeded, the performance of comparable traditional investments. This is on both an absolute and a risk-adjusted basis, across asset classes and over time, based on our review of US-based Mutual Funds and Separately Managed Accounts (SMAs).

- Sustainable equity Mutual Funds had equal or higher median returns and equal or lower volatility than traditional funds for 64% of the periods examined.

- There is a positive relationship between corporate investment in sustainability and stock price and operational performance, based on a review of existing studies.

- Long-term annual returns of one index comprising firms scoring highly on environmental, social and governance criteria exceeded the S&P 500 by 45 basis points since its inception in 1990.[2]

- Manager selection is crucial for sustainable and traditional investments alike.

Morgan Stanley
Institute for Sustainable Investing

Executive Summary

This study set out to analyze potential performance and risk differences between sustainable and traditional investments.

We reviewed a range of studies on sustainable investment performance and examined performance data for 10,228 open-end mutual funds and 2,874 Separately Managed Accounts (SMAs) based in the United States and denominated in US dollars. In the scope of our review, we ultimately found that **investing in sustainability has usually met, and often exceeded, the performance of comparable traditional investments. This is on both an absolute and a risk-adjusted basis, across asset classes and over time.**

More specifically, when investors are deciding whether to pursue a sustainable investing strategy, they should consider the following:

- Sustainable Equity Mutual Funds had equal or higher median returns and equal or lower median volatility for 64% of the periods examined over the last 7 years, compared to their traditional counterparts. (Figure 2).
- Sustainable SMAs had equal or higher median returns for 36% of the periods examined and equal or lower median volatility for 72% of the periods examined, over the last 7 years, compared to their traditional counterparts. On a risk-adjusted basis, sustainable SMAs performed closely inline with their traditional counterparts (Figure 5).
- Sustainable Mutual Funds and SMAs had a tighter return and volatility dispersion than their traditional peers (Figures 3, 4, 6).
- Individual Firms that actively pursue improvements in environmental, social and governance metrics also tend to have *lower costs of capital* and higher *operational* and *stock price performance*.[3]
- A 2011 Harvard study found, that given a $1 investment in 1993 in a value-weighted portfolio of high sustainability versus low sustainability firms, the high sustainability portfolio would have grown to $22.60 by 2010, while the low sustainability portfolio would have only reached $15.40, a difference of over 46%.[4]
- Benchmark performance of the MSCI KLD 400 Social Index, which includes firms meeting high Environmental, Social and Governance (ESG) standards, has outperformed the S&P 500 on an annualized basis by 45 basis points since its inception (10.14%, compared to 9.69% for the S&P 500; July 1990 - Dec. 2014).[5]

Ultimately, investors should remember that *manager selection is crucial*; there is a high dispersion of returns and volatility across the spectrum of sustainable and traditional investment strategies alike.

Methodology

To develop a clearer picture of the relative performance of sustainable investments to their traditional peers, our review focused on three broad areas:

- Individual Firm Performance. We reviewed a body of studies and meta studies that assessed the impact of sustainability on financial and market performance of individual firms.
- Benchmark Performance. We examined how the MSCI 400 KLD Social Index[6], an index of firms selected for their relative strength in sustainability metrics, performed against broader industry benchmarks.
- Investment Fund Performance. We used publicly-available data from Morningstar to assess open-end mutual fund performance, and data from Informa PSN to assess SMA performance. Performance was comparatively assessed using total returns for mutual funds and gross returns for SMAs, based on the availability of data. Risk was assessed using volatility (standard deviation). Our review used 7 years of calendar and trailing data, across both equity and fixed income. 10 year data could not be fairly assessed and was excluded due to a low number of sustainable funds in existence at the time. To reduce the potential for error, we compared sustainable and traditional investment performance between peers within the same Morningstar category or Informa asset class. We only included asset classes where there were *at least 4 sustainable funds or SMAs* with continuously available data over the last 7 years.

We wanted to review the performance of sustainable investments from these three perspectives; to arrive at a synthesized view that would be beneficial for asset owners and managers, institutional and retail investors and corporate management.

Defining Sustainability

We define sustainability as a commitment to economic well-being for both the present and the future, balancing society's needs today with the demands of tomorrow. Sustainability encompasses behaviors, processes, tools and technologies that can be perpetuated and replicated in ways that achieve economic, social or environmental benefits. We see sustainable investing as the practice of mobilizing capital to businesses that engage in these behaviors and practices.

This paper is published by the Morgan Stanley Institute for Sustainable Investing. The Morgan Stanley Institute for Sustainable Investing is dedicated to accelerating mainstream adoption of sustainable investing by developing innovative and scalable finance solutions to address global challenges, seeking both competitive financial returns and positive societal impact. The Institute is committed to industry-leading work that combines Morgan Stanley's tradition of excellence in client service with cutting-edge approaches to investment. For more information about the Morgan Stanley Institute for Sustainable Investing, visit http://www.morganstanley.com/sustainableinvesting. Kosh Patel was the principal author of this report.

Advocacy: An Important Function of Sustainable Fund Families

C alvert Funds are featured because of their robust commitment to advocacy. Other sustainable fund families may also advocate for progressive changes in corporate practices at companies being considered for investment purposes.

Potential investors should carefully consider investment objectives, risks, charges and expenses of the investment company when contemplating an investment in any particular fund. This information can be found in the prospectus or the summary prospectus for the funds in which you are interested. **Prospectuses can be downloaded from Calvert.com.** *Make sure to read the prospectus carefully before investing.*

Fund Advocacy in Practice

Calvert Funds, possibly the mutual fund family with the longest history of Socially Responsible Investing (SRI)-focused fund management, makes shareholder advocacy from a Socially Responsible perspective a centerpiece of its investing philosophy. The following is a 2013 statement from their website regarding this important topic:

PROXY VOTING. As company shareholders, Calvert votes on issues of corporate governance and social responsibility at annual meetings. We take our responsibility seriously and vote each proxy in a manner consistent with the financial and social objectives of our Funds, in support of most sustainable and responsible shareholder resolutions. Calvert's Global Proxy Voting Guidelines integrate corporate governance and corporate social responsibility into what Calvert calls a "sustainable governance" model that it shares with other mutual fund companies.

SHAREHOLDER RESOLUTIONS. A shareholder with $2,000 of company stock, held for one year, can file a resolution calling on a company to take a particular action, such as changing a company policy or producing a report on a particular issue of concern. If not settled favorably and withdrawn beforehand, these resolutions may come to a vote in front of all shareholders at the company's annual meeting. In 1986, Calvert Social Investment Fund (CSIF) became the first mutual fund to file a shareholder resolution with the Angelica Corporation on labor/management issues. Calvert routinely files or co-files up to three dozen resolutions each year with a wide range of companies on our priority objectives.

WORKING IN COALITIONS. Often we partner with other investors and Non-Governmental Organizations (NGOs) to advance common objectives. We believe there is power in numbers and in more company shares when we bring voices and interests to the table with different perspectives yet common objectives. We have greater leverage to work for Environment, Social Justice and Corporate Governance (ESG)-related improvements when we work through coalitions, whether by co-filing shareholder resolutions, engaging in company-specific or broader industry-wide multi-stakeholder dialogue, joint research or public policy platforms.

DIALOGUE WITH COMPANY EXECUTIVES. We regularly initiate conversations with management both as part of our social research process and corporate engagement program. After becoming a shareholder, we continue our dialogue with management through periodic calls, letters, and meetings. Through our interactions, we gain a sharper sense of the company's commitments, performance and challenges, and press for improvement in specific areas of concern. While our first responsibility on behalf of our shareholders is to engage with companies that we own, we have stepped up our dialogue with companies that do not currently pass all of Calvert's ESG criteria as many have begun to address corporate responsibility and sustainability issues more seriously over the last several years.

MULTI-STAKEHOLDER DIALOGUES. Calvert participates in issue or industry specific standard-setting exercises, working with other investors, corporations and members of civil society to formulate best practices or principles for new and challenging corporate responsibility issues. Such exercises present efficient and effective ways to raise standards in an entire industry. For example, Calvert participated in the two-year dialogue with Yahoo!, Google and Microsoft together with other SRIs, human rights NGOs and academic experts that produced the Global Network Initiative — the new standard launched in late 2008 that addresses the corporate responsibility of internet service providers to respect freedom of expression and the right to privacy in their operations around the world.

PUBLIC POLICY INITIATIVES. Calvert engages in public policy issues that are directly relevant to corporate responsibility and sustainability, and in turn to the economic interests of shareholders. We send comment letters to the SEC that attempt to reinforce certain shareholder rights, meet with policy-makers to encourage action on energy and climate change, and testify before congressional committees on areas of focus. For example, we testified on behalf of Sudan divestment to the U.S. Senate Banking Committee, and the Texas House of Representatives in 2007.

PUBLISHING RESEARCH REPORTS. Calvert produces industry and issue reports to contribute to the debate regarding best practices. We also use these reports, which benchmark company performance on key ESG issues, in our engagement with individual companies.

For example, we worked with the environmental and investor group CERES to produce the first-ever analysis of the carbon disclosure of S&P 500 companies in early 2007, and produced on our own, major reports in 2008 focusing on the green building practices of the U.S. homebuilding industry and the diversity policies and practices of the 600+ companies in the Calvert Social Index.

We then use these research reports as advocacy platforms from which we file or co-file shareholder resolutions, initiative dialogue with company management and publicize our findings.

In addition to deploying this combination of tools, we also reinforce our shareholder advocacy through public statements on the Calvert website and through the media to focus public attention on a particular company or issue.

Different approaches for different funds

For the **Signature Strategies**™ portfolios, Calvert's advocacy focuses on select companies with four strategic advocacy priorities guiding our company-specific and cross-sector activities:

- Environment and climate change,
- Human rights, labor rights and Indigenous Peoples' rights,
- Diversity and women,
- Governance and disclosure.

For **Solution Strategies**™ portfolios, which selectively invest in companies that produce products and services geared toward solving some of today's most pressing environmental and sustainability challenges, Calvert's advocacy focuses on issues specific to the sector:

- Advocacy related to the Calvert Global Alternative Energy Fund focuses on governance and environmental issues.
- Advocacy related to the Calvert Global Water Fund focuses on access to water and human rights issues, as well as transparency, disclosure and community relations.

For **SAGE Strategies**™ portfolios, Calvert's advocacy involves enhanced engagement with key companies that do not meet all of our Signature Strategies portfolios' ESG criteria, focused on the most salient risks and opportunities for those companies in their industry contexts. For these companies, we use the full combination of our engagement and shareholder advocacy tools, emphasizing direct company and multi-stakeholder dialogues and also including proxy voting and shareholder resolutions.

APPENDIX C

Investor Risk-Tolerance Questionnaire

The following questions are intended to measure your attitude toward risk as it applies to your investment goal.

Check one response for each statement:

I am prepared to sacrifice some safety for higher returns.

_____ Agree   _____ Disagree

_____ Somewhat agree   _____ Somewhat disagree

I am willing to accept some risk in an effort to stay ahead of inflation.

_____ Agree   _____ Disagree

_____ Somewhat agree   _____ Somewhat disagree

I am willing to accept fluctuating returns in order to achieve my goal.

_____ Agree   _____ Disagree

_____ Somewhat agree   _____ Somewhat disagree

From time to time I can tolerate negative returns.

_____ Agree   _____ Disagree

_____ Somewhat agree   _____ Somewhat disagree

I am willing to accept higher volatility to achieve above average returns.

_____ Agree   _____ Disagree

_____ Somewhat agree   _____ Somewhat disagree

Investment Objectives

The following questions should be answered in regard to the assets intended for this specific account only.

Your objectives and time horizon are crucial in determining an appropriate strategy for your portfolio.

A longer time horizon can take advantage of market cycles by using a more aggressive approach.

A shorter time horizon requires a more conservative strategy, which is less likely to be subject to large fluctuations.

What is your primary investment goal?

_____	Capital Appreciation	_____	Capital Preservation
_____	Capital Appreciation with Current Income	_____	Other

What is the expected time horizon of the account?

_____	3 Years	_____	15 Years
_____	5 Years	_____	20 Years
_____	10 Years	_____	Greater than 20 Years

If generating income is required from this account, when will the income be required?

_____	Immediately	_____	15 Years
_____	3 Years	_____	20 Years
_____	5 Years	_____	Greater than 20 Years
_____	10 Years		

What is the federal income tax rate on earnings from all sources?

_____	0% Tax deferred (IRA, Qualified Plans, etc.)				
_____	10%	_____	28%	_____	Other
_____	15%	_____	33%	_____	_____
_____	25%	_____	35%		

Is tax sensitive investing a primary goal?

_____ Yes   _____ No

How much do you plan to invest in the account?

$_____

How much money are you currently saving on an annual basis?

$_____

The portfolio we recommend for you may fluctuate over the short term.

Hypothetically, if you invested $100,000 and your account was performing in line with world financial markets and lost value during the year, at what point would you sell?

_____ I would not sell   _____ $80,000
_____ $90,000   _____ Less than $80,000

What is your approximate yearly household income? Or, what is your approximately yearly revenue? Include salary, bonuses, commission, pension plan distributions (excluding one time lump sum distributions), Social Security, interest and dividends earned, and all other income:

$_____

_____ Under 50k   _____ 200 k to 500k
_____ 50k to 100k   _____ Over 500k
_____ 100k to 200k

How much do you expect your household income (or revenue) to change over the next three years?

_____ Within 5% up or down   _____ Increase 5% to 20%
_____ Decrease 5% to 20%   _____ Increase greater than 20%
_____ Decrease greater than 20%

How much do you expect your household (or business) expenses to change over the next three years?

_____	Within 5% up or down	_____	Decrease 5% to 20%
_____	Decrease greater than 20%	_____	Increase 5% to 20%
_____	Increase greater than 20%		

What is the total current market value of all of your assets (or plan/ corporate assets)?

$_____

What is the total value of all your outstanding liabilities (or plan/ corporate liabilities)?

$_____

If you needed $10,000 due to an unexpected financial obligation, would you have to redeem form this account?

_____ Yes   _____ No

J. Patrick Costello, CFP®, CLU

CA Insurance License #0B33627
Certified Financial Planner™
Chartered Life Underwriter

Green River Sustainable Financial Services

321 San Anselmo Avenue
San Anselmo, CA 94960

PH: (415) 453-6000
FAX: (415) 520-0299
CELL: (415) 710-3978
EMAIL: PCostello@protectedInvestors.com

J. Patrick Costello is a Registered Representative of Cambridge Investment Research, Inc. Securities are offered solely by Cambridge Investment Research, Inc., Member FINRA/SIPC, a Broker Dealer. Advisory services provided through Cambridge Investment Research Advisors, Inc., located at 1776 Pleasant Plain Rd., Fairfield, IA 52556 (800) 777-6080. Cambridge and Green River Financial Services are unaffiliated. J. Patrick Costello is insurance licensed in the State of CA, License #OB33627.

www.ingramcontent.com/pod-product-compliance
Lightning Source LLC
Chambersburg PA
CBHW042310210326
41598CB00041B/7343